WILLIE, a Girl from a Town Called Dallas

Willie as a bride, September 19, 1912

WILLIE, a Girl from a Town Called Dallas

By

WILLIE NEWBURY LEWIS

Texas A&M University Press
COLLEGE STATION

Library of Congress Cataloging in Publication Data

Lewis, Willie Newbury.
Willie, a girl from a town called Dallas.

1. Lewis, Willie Newbury. 2. Lewis, William J., 1870–1960. 3. Dallas (Tex.)—Biography. 4. Ranchers' wives—Texas—Dallas—Biography. 5. Ranchers—Texas—Dallas—Biography. I. Title.
F394.D2153L494 1984 976.4'281206'0924 [B] 83-18081
ISBN 0-89096-175-1

The information in chapter 6 on the history of the Spur Ranch is taken from William Curry Holden, *The Spur Ranch* (Boston: Christopher Publishing House, 1934). The discussion in chapter 7 of "free grass" ranches and water rights is from Willie Newbury Lewis, *Tapadero: The Making of a Cowboy* (Austin: University of Texas Press, 1972), pp. 17, 100.

Manufactured in the United States of America
FIRST EDITION

Illustrations

Preface

FOR you to understand this story you must first become more or less familiar with the wide expanse of land known geographically as Texas. In some respects it is a violent land, with its bitter cold, extreme heat, tornadic winds, cloudbursts, and droughts. Added to this, the terrain of Texas is wide and varied—there are mountains, forests, prairies, plains, extremely rich farmland, a seacoast, and, underneath, untold amounts of oil, gas, and coal. It is important to remember that the nature of the land forms the character of the man bred upon it.

From the beginning of my marriage, I was interested in the portion of Texas known as the Panhandle, which at that time was the setting for many huge ranches. Because of this, I traveled far and wide, interviewing the old families who had followed the Indians as the region's first settlers. My research resulted in an informal history of the Panhandle.

Since my husband objected seriously to my writing, I did not attempt a second book until after his death. At that time I wrote *Tapadero: The Making of a Cowboy*, the story of Will's early life and his fascination with the beautiful Texas prairies and the art of cattle raising.

The task of writing this story, for which I was not especially trained, required endless assistance. I wish to thank the following: Frank Wardlaw, who introduced me to the literary world; Kirk Burbage, the Southern Methodist University student who served as both my eyes and my first stenographer, and whom I came to regard almost as an adopted grandchild; Miriam Cash, my friend and permanent stenographer; and Vivian Checkley, my intelligent and interested nurse, who worked with me endlessly on the final revisions.

WILLIE, a Girl from a Town Called Dallas

1

I am almost 92 years old. Although I do not consider old age, with its attendant infirmities, the ideal state, it does offer one very valuable compensation: the ability to take a long backward perspective of a life that has lasted almost a century.

My marriage to Will Lewis should have been a beautiful experience because he, like my father, was a fine and honorable man. But the wide differences in our ages and personalities presented obstacles too great to be easily overcome, and disaster came close on more than one occasion.

In recent months I have begun to wonder if much of the responsibility did not lie with me, because I was a deeper thinker than Will. I should have known that my first duty was to force myself to become familiar with the industry he loved so dearly and the unusual terrain upon which it was conducted.

I also should never have overlooked the fact that Will had been forced to go to work for himself at the early age of sixteen, that he often traveled the range alone for days at a time, that most of his life was spent with rough cowboys, and that he rarely saw a woman outside of his family. As a result, companionship was not one of the requirements he sought in marriage.

Being a confirmed Victorian, Will believed that a woman's function in life was limited to a few specific fields, such as being a man's sexual partner, the mother of his children, the manager of his household, and last, but of much importance, the means by which he displayed his success to the outside world. By the time I learned all this it was too late, and I had withdrawn into my own little shell to search for my life fulfillment elsewhere.

This is the story of the marriage of a forty-two-year-old man, who moved to the frontier of Texas as a boy of fourteen, and a highly sheltered and much-loved Dallas girl of twenty. Willie—that is my name, although neither my father nor my husband ever called me anything but Bill. I was born in a cottage on Saint Louis Street in a part of town commonly known as the Cedars. In the early 1890s Dallas, although the fastest-growing community in Texas, was little more than an unsophisticated, overgrown small town. Like Masten Street and certain parts of Ross, McKinney, and Maple avenues, the Cedars was considered one of its better residential districts. Ervay Street was a block and a half to the west of my home, Harwood Street a block to the east, and the business district within easy walking distance.

Even in the better homes, gas and electricity were not accepted parts of daily living. Houses were heated by fireplaces or by large wood-burning stoves, and air conditioning was as yet unknown. The summers thus seemed much hotter than they do today. Some respite from the heat was achieved at night by keeping the windows open, but during the day when the sun glared down, windows were closed within an inch of the sill, and the shades were drawn. Everyone who was not working attempted to sleep during the hot afternoons. The sound of the neighborhood yardman's lawnmower, accompanied by the song of the cicadas, or katydids, as everyone called them, was prevalent everywhere.

Lamps were the commonest form of lighting. In my home there hung from the center of the living room ceiling a chandelier-like contraption composed of a central container for coal oil and five or six adjoining burners resembling candelabra. My father had a special stick that enabled him to apply a lighted match to the tips of the burners, and the lighting ceremony took place each evening at the approach of dusk.

Another ritual—though more of a weekly chore than the daily routine it is today—was bathing. According to some reminiscences, there were practically no bathtubs at that time, even in the finer homes, but I have no recollection of bathing in any way other than in a stationary, tin-lined tub in a bathroom.

Transportation at the turn of the century was also quite different from the streamlined systems of today. The three main streets of the business section—Elm, Main, and Commerce—were paved with bois d'arc blocks, and the other streets, having remained in their natural state, became a muddy slush when it rained. Crossing for pedestrians was possible only at intersections where a walk of planks was constructed by laying two wide planks together and placing a third on top in the center where the lower two were joined. The well-to-do in town kept horses and carriages, while the rest walked or hired a hack—or a victoria, if the occasion demanded more dignity.

In time, Dallas installed a transit system. The streetcars were mule-drawn, entirely open vehicles with a long bench on either side of the car for seating. The streetcars would follow certain routes on what were loosely termed "belt-lines." Often on Sundays, my parents would give my playmate and me a nickel apiece to amuse ourselves with a long ride.

When the recently invented telephone arrived in Dallas, it was a clumsy affair that hung on the wall. At the side was a handle that, when cranked, attracted the attention of the operator, who then made the proper connection. Residential telephones were few, and even many business houses considered them unnecessary.

There were, of course, no supermarkets, and the grocery stores offered mainly staples such as flour, sugar, meal, coffee, and meat. Vegetables usually were procured from the vegetable man, who made daily rounds in his wagon. It was not considered good form for the mistress of the house to go out to the wagon to select her own vegetables, but my mother paid little heed to this edict, since our one maid was usually busy at more strenuous tasks.

Many prominent families lived in the Cedars, but only a few were friends of my parents. The heads of these families were older, well-established businessmen, and my parents were very young. Later, my father came to know the heads of these families very well.

My father, Henry Lee Newbury, while in his early twenties had moved with my mother, Anna Hearn Newbury, and their small son, Orren, from Pilot Point to Dallas. Father had accepted a permanent position with the Trezevant and Cochran Insurance Company, for which he had been working as an outside agent. Through the advice of Sam P. Cochran, one of the partners in the company, he later moved to a better position as cashier in the City National Bank. Eventually my father left the bank to go into business for himself. During all my younger years he was a shoe merchant, and his original store was on Elm, near Griffin. Later, he expanded to include a store in Fort Worth, the shoe department in the original Titche-Goettinger store, and a small store for used merchandise farther out on Elm.

At the time of my parents' marriage my mother belonged to the Baptist church, but, in the belief that a family should worship together, left to join her husband in the Presbyterian church. He later became a deacon, and my mother served as the principal of the children's Sunday school department.

It was not my quick-tempered father but my timid, quiet, and retiring mother who set the tone of our family life. Whatever the circumstances, she continued to occupy herself with interests equally enjoyable with or without companionship. She loved music, the theater, literature, and flowers, as well as simple handicrafts such as crocheting and china painting. I still have on my desk one of her productions, a charming hand-painted mug, decorated with the face of a monk. She also loved and knew a great deal about birds in Texas and often spoke for enjoyment to groups of women interested in the subject.

My mother had what gardeners call a green thumb. Her approach to growing flowers was more that of an amateur botanist than that of the casual interest of a housewife. Nothing, even when in full bloom, was removed from our garden to brighten the interior. Like many other Dallas women, she had a backyard flower pit in which her flowers grew during the winter months. This crude greenhouse was formed by digging a hole of sufficient depth and size to accommodate two or more wooden steps for the flowers and smaller steps for an entrance into the pit. Above the pit was a high back wall and slanting side walls, to which were attached by hinges a pair of glass windows. These windows, which could be opened or closed as necessary, served not only to protect the plants from winter weather but also to admit the warm rays of the sun.

For years, Mama continued an intermittent correspondence with a large Philadelphia nursery in order to send for some unfamiliar plant she had noticed in their catalogue. I remember my own amusement years later upon seeing a landscape architect's suggestion for a border plant for my formal garden on Belfort Place. "So this Jap grass is something new?" I inquired. Then I added, "Not to me. It's been growing in clumps in Mama's yard for years. I simply didn't know what it was called."

My mother was among twelve women invited to a luncheon to discuss the formation of a local garden club, and this luncheon was the initial step in the formation of the Dallas Garden Club (part of the Dallas Woman's Club). When the club published its first garden book, she contributed the chapter on classification of wild flowers. Later she was consulted by the Texas Highway Department on the subject of developing the growth of wild flowers along the state's highways.

The family home was run in about the same manner as the greenhouse. Mama was an excellent housekeeper and set a good table. I remember well the hours my mother spent each fall making quart after quart of mincemeat for winter pies. I still serve at my table today the kind of charlotte russe and snow pudding that my mother used to serve.

As comfortable and homelike as our house was, Mama was completely disinterested in beautifying it. Whatever she purchased had a functional, not a decorative, purpose, and the day of the professional decorator was still far away. The family did, however, possess and enjoy some beautiful things:

a silver tea service that had belonged to the Newbury family, beautiful knives, forks, teaspoons, and tablespoons. The tablespoons, molded from melted silver dollars, were especially prized because they had been a wedding gift at Grandpa Newbury's postwar wedding. Their unusual method of manufacture came about because no silver was available for purchase following the Civil War. We also owned an entire set of Haviland china decorated with violets, which, however, was used only on special occasions.

My mother was a member of the Saint Cecilia Choral Club, an organization promoted and managed by a busy little woman, Mrs. Jules D. Roberts. On occasion the choral society gave concerts, but its most important function was to sponsor annually in Dallas the appearances of such renowned artists as Ignace Paderewski. I accompanied my parents to the concerts and was often taken backstage to be introduced to the artist of the evening.

My mother also belonged to two neighborhood book clubs. The book club of that era enabled its members to keep abreast of numerous current novels through the purchase of only one. There were always twelve members, and after reading her own novel, each member passed it on at the first of the month to another specified member, probably her nearest neighbor. The variety of novels that arrived monthly at our house greatly encouraged my love of reading.

Both my parents loved the theater. When the old opera house burned in 1901, a new and much larger one was constructed on Commerce Street, for Dallas has always been theater oriented. Even in those early days, the best talent from New York was available on occasion, giving Dallas patrons the privilege of seeing such performances as Richard Mansfield in *Monsieur Beaucaire*, Joseph Jefferson in *Rip Van Winkle*, and James O'Neill in *The Count of Monte Cristo*. I shed copious tears over Bonaparte's farewell to Josephine and thrilled with teenage delight over fat old Chauncey Alcott's rendition of Irish love songs. As a result, the theater has never lost its fascination for me.

At that time, Dallas society was loosely divided into two

sets, the "church set" and the "society set." My mother and father belonged to the former. Whether my mother's timidity was the result of temperament or of her forced adjustment, while immature, from the intimate circle of a small town into the more sophisticated life of Dallas is an undecided question. Although pretty, well mannered, well educated, and stylishly dressed, she had little self-confidence. As a result, Society with a capital S never appealed to her. Her one concession to formal society was to hire each fall a specially designed pleasure carriage for two known as a victoria, and gowned in her best, with calling cards in hand, to make the rounds of certain matrons' homes. When I became old enough, I often accompanied her.

Except for their love of the theater, music, reading, and the church, my mother and father were dissimilar in taste, temperament, and personality. I was quite old before I realized how much my father, even though somewhat puritanical, must have sacrificed to live a life in certain respects unsuited to him. He was by no means gregarious, but he both liked and needed the company of others. A friend at the City National Bank once invited him to become a member of the Idlewild Club. He would have enjoyed the membership very much, but was forced to decline because of his wife's vehement objection.

On the serious side, my father was a real Christian according to the Christianity of a hundred years ago. To him, the Bible was composed not of folk tales handed down from generation to generation by word of mouth, but of the written word of God. The Ten Commandments were to be followed to the letter. He accepted fully the bibilical assertion that Jews were God's chosen people, and he permitted no criticism of Jews or Jewish jokes in his presence. Living next door to our cottage were a Jewish widow and her three daughters, with whom we were on the friendliest of terms. As strictly religious as he was, in some respects my father was very broad-minded for his day. When I asked, for example, to go with a neighboring youngster to Mass at her Catholic church, he did not object.

Another example of his tolerant outlook was when Albert, the black neighborhood yardman who cut our grass and kept the flower beds in order, came to him seeking the solution to a problem. Albert was unable, he said, to support his family on his present wages, although he worked steadily. Recently, he had been offered a well-paying job as bartender in a saloon. Was it my father's opinion that he should refuse or accept the job? Although a strict prohibitionist, my father answered, "It would be wrong, Albert, for me to become a bartender, but your first duty is to your family, so take the job."

One spring, a black man of about fifty badly molested a little white girl, who was scarcely more than a baby. All of Dallas was deeply aroused, the whites over the nature of the crime and the blacks over the nature of the possible consequences. After a week or so, the alleged criminal was found and placed in jail to await trial. Early in the morning of the first day of the trial, a crowd of about two hundred men gathered at the courthouse, forced their way into the courtroom, overpowered the deputies, and started toward the door with the defendant. As they moved, a rope came sailing through the window, and angry cries and shouts were heard from below. "Throw him out, throw him out, we'll string him up." Very quickly, the rope was tied securely, and the prisoner was hurled through the window and to the ground below. He fell face down, landing on his head. The blow left him either unconscious or dead.

The determined mob did not stop to investigate, but hastily started to drag the victim up Main Street, continuing on its grim course until it reached Akard Street. There, about two years earlier, the Elks had erected a large iron arch of welcome to convention members. The apparent culprit was quickly hanged from the arch. By this time, the crowd had grown to about five thousand and had decided to move on to the jail and wreak the same vengeance on two other prisoners; but, unfortunately for the mobsters and fortunately for the prisoners, the police had spirited them away a few hours before.

Long before this violent act concluded, my father locked the door of his store in protest and started for home. He was deeply affected by all of this, surprised that five thousand mobsters lived among the good people of Dallas and that mob violence would ever be allowed by the police. He firmly believed in equal justice for all and strongly opposed mob rule. Father was grieved that once again the old dilemma of whites against blacks still existed and continued to ask, "What kind of people do such things?"

I have wondered often during the last few years if my early life did not represent the kind of life so many of today's insecure youngsters are searching for. My parents were rarely absent from home. Roxie, our maid and cook, had been with us for such a long while that she was considered a part of the family. My days were filled with playing with the neighborhood children, attending school, and, later, with taking music lessons. Although I had no musical talent, I spent years studying both the violin and the piano. I was always included in the outside activities of my parents, and there were always certain tasks to do at home. I helped my brother rake the leaves that fell from the large cottonwood tree in the front yard. On Saturdays I had to attempt to remove, either with soap and water or gasoline, the spots from my older brother's long trousers and to press them, for as yet there were neither cleaning establishments nor fluids for home use. This duty was one that was especially distasteful for me.

From the beginning, my parents intended that their children have the best possible education. I started school at the Columbian Public School on Akard Street, but at the end of the second year I was placed in Miss Cowart's School for Girls. I can well remember that momentous morning when my mother dressed me in the sort of uniform I was to wear through all my younger school years: a plaid woolen dress over which was worn a beruffled, clean, and starched white apron. I also wore long black stockings and, during the winter months, heavy underwear. The wearing of this apparel began on a certain date in the fall and ended on a certain date in the spring, regardless of the temperature.

Cowart Hall, as the girls' school was called, was located in a narrow, three-story brick building on Browder Street, in the Cedars. The arrangement of the rooms was somewhat unusual, and all floors had the same floor plan. On the left-hand side were an entrance hall and a stairway. On the right were two average-size rooms with a smaller room in the back. The back room on the first floor served as a kitchen. The students often heated soup there and ate cheese and crackers, as well as cream puffs from a bakery around the corner on Ervay Street. Except for the kitchen, all the rooms on the first and second floors were used as classrooms. The third floor was used exclusively for art and Delsarte lessons. (Since you may never have heard of Delsarte, the dictionary's definition may be necessary: "A system of calisthentics patterned on the theories of François Delsarte [1811–71], a French teacher of dramatic and musical expression.") Miss Cowart's purpose, however, was not exactly the purpose of Monsieur Delsarte. Hers was to instruct her students in the art of entering a room gracefully, employing their hands unobtrusively, and reading and reciting well. Miss Cowart's sole interest in this kind of training was to prepare her girls for the specific role she expected them to play in later life.

Most of the pupils at Cowart Hall were the daughters of parents with only one career in mind for their girls—that of marriage. Miss Lora, as we called Miss Cowart, offered the kind of education that suited that goal. In addition to the basics, she also emphasized good manners and good taste. Lessons in Latin and French began in the first grade. She taught both languages well, but unknowingly pronounced both improperly. Students conjugated Latin verbs and eventually progressed to the translation of excerpts from such works as Cicero's *Orations*, Vergil's *Aeneid*, and Ovid's *Metamorphoses*. I remember translating only one French work, Dumas's *La Tulip noire*.

About seventy-five students attended the school, but there was no grade classification. The girls were loosely grouped according to age rather than by position on the educational ladder. If there were ever any examinations, I have no memory of them.

We were taught to write not only legibly but in a beautiful Spencerian style. This sort of handwriting was slightly larger in form than most, slanting and extremely legible as well as attractive.

Great emphasis was placed on spelling and speaking English correctly. One of the teaching methods used was the simple "*i* before *e*" rhyme. The pupils also learned how to diagram sentences and to parse. Consequently, no Cowart Hall girl was ever known to make the mistake of saying "Somebody did something to so-and-so and *I*."

Familiarity with English and French classics, as well as American, was considered necessary. We read Shakespeare frequently. Miss Lora was a member of the prestigious Dallas Shakespeare Club, and on one special occasion her students performed *A Midsummer Night's Dream* for the club on the spacious lawn of Mrs. Burgher, a club member.

Besides Miss Cowart, there were several other teachers. One of these, whom I remember as a mousy little old maid, caused great concern at school when she married one George Clifton Edwards, a supposed socialist. Most Dallasites knew little about the nature of socialist activities and even less about the meaning of socialism, but, being Victorians, were terrified by the word.

School, in general, was a very happy experience. In addition to activities at school, the students were occasionally drawn into unusual happenings outside. For instance, the Trinity River had not yet been dammed and diked sufficiently to prevent flooding. During one very damaging flood, many business houses were destroyed or ruined. In the afternoon of that eventful day classes were dismissed, and, with Miss Cowart acting as sergeant, the entire school was led on a march down Commerce Street to view the spreading waters and the little boat that was plying back and forth between Oak Cliff and Dallas.

Each spring a country picnic was planned, and once again

the seventy-five students, lunch boxes in hand, rode the interurban halfway to Fort Worth, disembarked, and picnicked in the field of the first nearby farm offering a shade tree or two.

In addition to all the events school brought to my life, I was busy in other ways. Even though only nine or ten, I was expected during this time to come directly home from school and, for the remainder of the afternoon, whip lace on petticoats, "drawers," and nightgowns. In this way, I became fairly proficient with the needle. A few Dallasites wore silk lingerie specially made for them by the nuns in the convent, but my mother and I wore only homemade cotton underwear, the products of a dressmaker who earned a dollar and a half a day working for the family several weeks each spring and fall.

Every summer my mother and I went to visit my grandparents in Pilot Point. These visits were great events for me, for I was usually allowed to stay on after my mother had returned home. Because traveling was not an everyday experience, the trips were very much anticipated. My mother always wore her best underwear in order to look like a gentlewoman in case of a serious accident on the train.

My maternal grandparents, Grandpa and Grandma Hearn, lived on the corner of an entire block of land not far from the downtown square upon which stood my grandfather's general store. The house was large and rambling with several bedrooms upstairs, but it was neither a cottage nor a two-story house in the accepted sense. A banistered veranda extended across the front and around one side. Beside the etched-glass entrance door stood two large pink oleanders, which bloomed throughout the summer. During the winter months, these plants were moved indoors. There was an entrance hall, with a dining room at one side, a parlor and a sitting room at the other. On the dining room wall hung a large, framed copy of the Hearn family tree. In the sitting room was an oversized window where I often sat when noon approached in order to see Grandpa as he walked home from the store for the main meal of the day. Both he and Grandma were strict prohibitionists, but she made an excellent blackberry wine, for "medicinal purposes only." I can still see and hear my handsome grandfather as he stepped through the door, removed his hat, wiped his brow, and said, "It is very hot outside, Mattie, and today's walk has tired me excessively. Don't you think a little of your wine might make me feel better?" She never refused.

Their home was almost like a tiny farm in the center of town. There were stables, a garden, an orchard, and a large pasture for the horses and milk cows. I occasionally visited some distant cousins who lived across town, but my main companions were Grandma, as she busied herself around the house, or Stella Tompkins, who lived in the next block across the railroad tracks. Stella and I were constant playmates, playing first at her house and then at Grandma's. We always managed to stop long enough to play crossed pins on the railroad track. After laying the pins on the track, we would climb high on the embankment to wait until the wheels of the daily passenger train from Dallas had pressed the pins into tiny pairs of scissors. The engineer and the fireman came to know us and waved a friendly good-day in passing.

Mother and I always went dutifully to Grandfather Newbury's farm as well, but neither of us enjoyed it very much. My father's mother had died when he was a small boy, and his father had married a Nebraska woman to whom he had been engaged before moving to Texas. The engagement had been broken at the time of the Civil War, when he wrote her that, since he intended to make his permanent home in Texas, he felt it his duty to fight with the other Texans on the Confederate side. She returned his ring with the bitter comment that it was making her finger as black as she knew his heart had become. She was destined later, however, to become his second wife and the stepmother who reared my father and his beloved, short-lived little sister. She was, unfortunately, the kind of woman with whom neither my mother nor I felt comfortable, although she made every effort to be friendly.

Both she and Grandfather Newbury loved flowers. Grandfather had torn out a section of the dining room wall to add a glassed addition that served as a greenhouse. I always secretly watched the blossoming plants as we knelt for our pre-breakfast prayers. I can still hear the big bell that stood on a post outside the kitchen as it rang to call my grandfather to dinner and the hooting of owls that frightened me with their eerie night calls; and I can still see the beautiful handmade spool bed in which my mother and I always slept.

There were few trips of more importance than the summer vacations with grandparents. In 1900, however, my mother and I went to Brooklyn, New York, to visit an uncle of my father's. We made the trip by boat from Galveston on the Concho Line. As unusual as being on shipboard must have been, I have only two recollections of the week-long trip: one was the large schools of porpoises that playfully followed the ship through the day; the other, the small black boys who made a business of diving for the nickels and dimes that the passengers threw overboard while in port at Key West, Florida.

Uncle Henry lived on a block of brownstone fronts a short distance from Prospect Park. He had only two children, Frank and Ed, who were students at Cornell, but, happily for me, were home on vacation during my visit. The boys evidently enjoyed the unusual experience of having a girl in the house and played often with me. In later years, Frank became a vice-president of Westinghouse; Ed, vice-president of the Pennsylvania Railroad.

Most families in those days had some older relative living with them—a maiden great-aunt, a grandmother, or a grandfather. Although they did no actual work, the elders served the valuable purpose of willingly caring for the children when the parents were absent. Such arrangements are no longer common, and the life-style between generations is so different that neither the young nor the old are able to integrate happily into one household. Consequently, many of the older members of a family pass their last days in loneliness, and the youngsters lose the opportunity of living closely in a measure with the past, an experience that is often beneficial.

About the time I was eleven, various changes began to occur in my life. The two eldest daughters of our much-liked Jewish neighbors had married. Shortly after, their mother, Gaga, died. The youngest daughter, Bertha, was the only one left in their home, and she agreed to rent her house to us under the condition that she be allowed to remain there as our boarder until her contract with the public school where she taught had been fulfilled. Our cottage was quickly put on the market and sold, and we were soon settled in our new place of residence. It was a house of no great distinction but more comfortable and better suited to the needs of our family. It had a sitting room, parlor, dining room, and kitchen downstairs, and four large bedrooms upstairs.

Some months after this move, my father caught a cold that developed rapidly into pleurisy so severe that surgery was indicated. Dr. Leake, our family physician, was not only what is now called an internist, but was also an excellent surgeon. Dallas, although growing fast, was still a small town without the advantages of a city. Baylor, Saint Paul, and Parkland hospitals had not yet been developed. Dr. Leake was later to have a hospital of his own, but, at the time, it did not exist. Consequently, my father's surgery was performed in our home. After much scrubbing and disinfecting, the dining room was converted into an operating room, and the dining room table served as the operating table. The operation was most successful, and before long my father was back at work.

In January following my twelfth birthday, Dr. Leake was again on duty in our house, this time to deliver to my parents a second son, whom they named Edward Lee Newbury. "Lee," of course, was for my father, and "Edward" honored a most intimate friend, Ed Tennison, who was president of the City National Bank. I remember so well his bringing us an unusual gift during my father's illness, a sack containing several pieces of fruit resembling very oversized lemons or oranges. "These," he explained, "are in Dallas for the first time. They are something new and considered quite a delicacy. They are called grapefruit."

In the years that followed my brother Edward's birth, my

mother refused to leave home. I was not required to tend baby Edward often, but I have always felt very close to him, even though twelve years older, and he, in time, came to regard me as a sort of mother. Roxie had died, and Mother did not feel comfortable leaving the baby with the new cook. I have often wondered if this was not largely an excuse to prevent her from going to certain social events in which she was not interested. Had my father been a less moral man, he would have sought companionship elsewhere. Instead, he turned to me to accompany him to the places he would not have enjoyed alone.

Out on Second Avenue was Cycle Park, an open-air theater with a resident cast and a weekly change of program. Such a theater would have slight appeal today. It lacked both the fine acting and the attractive scenery demanded by more sophisticated audiences, as well as the bawdy allusions and blatant sex which certain people find amusing. Nevertheless, in the early twentieth century it was a popular place to go, and my father and I were regular patrons. Every week with keen enjoyment we watched badly acted melodrama based on such subjects as illicit or unrequited love. The wrongdoer, usually male, always received his just punishment; the victim, an equally just reward. My father, safe in the belief that I did not fully understand the subject matter, felt comfortable having me with him. At the beginning of the century, sex and the more serious aspects of life were relatively unknown to a girl in her early teens.

As I grew older, my father's unfounded belief that I was the smartest of his children continued. As far as he was able, he attempted to instill in me the business principles by which he operated. For instance, when he opened a personal account for me at Sanger Brothers, he reminded me that all bills were mailed out monthly, as a rule by the first of the month, and that they should be paid in full before the tenth. He believed that a man of character always owned his own home and, after the appearance of the automobile, his own car.

My experience with the Sanger Brothers charge account

gave me a certain amount of confidence about business that I had not previously had. During the past three or four years, for example, I had noticed that many people served uncooked vegetables not with the family dinner on the dinner plate, but on smaller plates, accompanied by a salad fork. I had been saving a certain part of my allowance to purchase such forks, knowing that they would be of no significant interest to my mother. I was certain that the salad forks could be bought at Sanger Brothers on my charge account, but I preferred that they come from the finest jewelers in town. Armed with my savings and the confidence given me by my Sanger's account, I made my way downtown to Linz Brothers. As I always did when I felt my finances to be of importance, even if only to myself, I asked to speak to one of the owners, Joe Linz, who was most pleasant. As soon as I had chosen the pattern and inquired as to the price, I discovered that my savings were not adequate for more than four or five of the dozen I wanted. I explained my dilemma, then asked if it would be possible for the store to hold the remainder until I was able to pay for them.

Mr. Linz quickly answered, "Why don't you take them all home today and pay the remaining balance at your convenience? That will be quite agreeable with me."

Knowing that this was against my father's principles, I thanked him and refused, returning home with only the ones paid for. Within a few months the dozen was complete. My mother's reaction was that I placed too much importance on things of unimportance, and my father thought perhaps my money could have been more wisely spent. I have felt many times since that my actions may unintentionally have embarrassed him greatly: he was a man of great pride, and his business was not doing too well at that time.

When I was about fourteen, my grandmother Hearn's eyesight failed, making it necessary for my grandparents to move to Dallas, where our family could help care for her. Grandpa, being well-to-do, sold his store and the home place in Pilot Point and bought a house large enough for our two families on the corner of Worth Street and Haskell Avenue. I was delighted with the move because I knew several girls in the neighborhood, the house was by far the largest I had ever lived in, and we had not only a cook and a manservant but also a carriage and a nice team of horses.

It required several months to get settled. As soon as everything was in order, my mother and I left for a two-week vacation and rest in Colorado. I shall never forget how frightened I was when I alighted from the little "cog train" to look down upon the world from Pike's Peak.

Returning to school, I discovered that a new teacher, Kate Wilson, who had recently received degrees from Wellesley and the Sorbonne and who was from the Oak Cliff section of Dallas, had been added to the staff. She was a superb English teacher, and it was from her that I acquired all of my basic knowledge of serious writing. Among my prized possessions are copies of *The Scarlet Letter*, *Pride and Prejudice*, and *The Marble Faun*, which I read under her guidance, all three marked over with such directions as "shows character," "indication of events to come," and "development of plot."

The following year, 1907, when I was about sixteen, Miss Cowart closed her school because of her age and poor health. In commemoration of the closing, Colonel Hughes, who had established the City National Bank and was a close friend of Miss Lora's family, offered the use of his country home for a week-long house party. It was a beautiful place, somewhere in the vicinity of the present-day Brook Hollow Golf Club. The house party was a significant experience for me, for one of the older girls taught me to dance the waltz and the two-step. Dancing was something that gave me a great deal of pleasure for many years.

In the fall, I entered Miss Holley's School for Girls. This experience was neither educational nor particularly pleasant. Few of my friends were there, because most of them had gone either to schools in the East or to the University at Austin. Although it would have been a financial strain for my parents, I am certain that I, too, could have gone away to school had I wished to go. I was not eager to leave, however, and my parents, like most other people, felt that higher education was not necessary for a girl.

Sometime during my last two years at Cowart Hall, my mother decided that a house large enough to require two servants was more than she cared to be burdened with. Whether my grandfather objected to my mother's plans is not known, but she finally persuaded him to sell and move with my family to a smaller cottage, purchased by my father, on Swiss Avenue. My mother was not too interested in the house except for its smaller size, but my father made interior improvements that made it attractive and livable. We also had a large lawn and very pleasant neighbors. We had not lived in the house more than a year when Grandmother died. Within a comparatively short time Grandfather married a very likable woman who had lived for years across from him in Pilot Point. After the wedding, they moved to Hillsboro.

The years of my girlhood were over, and a new period was beginning.

2

By 1910, Dallas had long since ceased to be the small town of my early childhood. The main streets, even in the residential districts, were paved with asphalt, all thoroughfares were electrically lighted, and the mule-drawn cars had been replaced by trolley cars. Having finished school, I had entered the state of "young ladyhood." I had been dating for several years under strict supervision as to where and with whom I went, and the hour by which I must return. The boys quickly learned whether a girl was a "nice girl," and, if so, she was not troubled by having to fight off amorous advances. I have never confessed to my grandchildren that I was first kissed on the evening I told their grandfather I would marry him. They would only laugh and think that, for once, I was lying to them. Now, in my early nineties, I am not certain that such complete abstinence from any form of sexual stimulation is the best path to follow in the long run, but I have no substitute to suggest.

The next few years of my life were filled with very happy memories. The family went once to Colorado, and when I was nearly grown, we went to California. The most interesting trip, however, was to Mexico City one summer when my mother and I traveled with Mrs. Roberts of the Saint Cecilia Choral Club and her mother, Mrs. Bryant, who was my music teacher. I was seventeen at the time, blonde, and different enough in appearance to be attractive to the men below the border. I had one very serious beau, Rodríguez, who at the time of my visit was attending the National University of Mexico, probably as a graduate student. He came from a prominent landed family in the northern province of Coahuila and seemed to have relatives all over Mexico. One cousin was at the Mexican West Point, which at that time occupied the famous old Chapultepec Castle. Another attended the cavalry officers' training school at Tlalpam, which is fairly close to Mexico City.

Rodríguez set out to show my mother and me the sights of Mexico City. On the day we visited the castle, the student band stood in readiness to play "My Old Kentucky Home" as we went through the gate into the courtyard. The young men at Tlalpam were mounted, so there were special equestrian exercises to see. All of this happened shortly before the end of Díaz's dictatorship. I am certain that great poverty and abuse of the peasants prevailed, but to visitors the city was gay and untroubled. There were band concerts in every park each day, and late in the afternoon, all upperclass women, beautifully gowned and hatted, were driven in their private carriages through the main streets of town. At funerals for the less wealthy, the deceased and his family and friends rode to the cemetery in a flower-bedecked streetcar. It was like a fascinating pageant.

Later that fall Rodríguez made the trip from Saltillo to Texas to see me, bringing gifts from his mother and sister. He was a very nice-looking young man, blond and blue-eyed, and I liked him well enough. Since I did not greet his unexpected visit with much enthusiasm, however, I never saw him again.

During the early years of dating, most young people dated in groups. One of the places frequented was the new Majestic Theater, which offered the best vaudeville shown anywhere. Everyone in my crowd saw the show on the same night and made certain that their tickets were on the last, or next to last, row.

On Sunday afternoons a girl and her best friends were prepared to "receive." First one group of two or three boys dropped in for a while and then moved on as various other groups made the rounds from one girl's house to another. As a rule, the favorites managed to arrive late so as to spend supper and the remainder of the evening with the girls of their preference.

All the dances were program dances, and a girl's date for the evening marked off as many dances as he wanted far in advance. A week or so ahead of time, the popular girls' programs were filled, and the first, second, or third extra dance positions on the card were promised to those who had failed to telephone, since every so often the orchestra would announce an extra. No hostess would have dreamed of giving a dance without inviting a sizable number of "stags," as the boys without dates were called.

3

I no longer remember the names of most of the young men with whom I went about a great deal. Only a few stand out in sharp silhouette, and I wonder often what my life would have been like, whether happier or not, had I married one of them—what sort of differences there might have been in the woman I eventually became.

I think often of Phil, with whom I went steady for a year. He had been sent from the North as district manager of a large eastern paint and paper company. He was well educated but not from an Ivy League college. He worked hard and was sufficiently ambitious to want to rise to a higher post in his company, but he had no overriding desire for great wealth. He was gentle of spirit, full of fun, and loved both life and me very much. Nothing of unusually good quality appeared in Dallas for which Phil did not procure tickets and make a date with me far in advance. I shall never forget seeing Anna Pavlova and Mondkin dance *Swan Lake*. It was my introduction to the art of ballet, and I still believe that I was far more thrilled than when fifty years later, on my first trip to London, I saw Fonteyn and Nureyev dance at Covent Garden. Dallas has always had excellent theater, and it was at a play with Phil that I experienced what I now recognize as the forerunner of women's lib. It was the performance of *A Doll's House*, by Ibsen, with Alla Nazimova as the star. I remember thinking at the time that the subject matter reminded me of one of Barrie's plays I particularly liked, *The Twelve Pound Look*. The chief interest in the story for me was that two men were the ones who were fighting for women's rights.

Phil liked sports as well as the theater; baseball was then the national sport, and Phil's favorite. We never missed a game, and he never failed to give me a flower that signified by its color the team of his choice. He cried when I told him I was going to make my debut, saying that he then knew I had no thought of marrying him and that he would never see me again because the hurt would heal faster that way. I missed him and the good times we had enjoyed together, but was not too upset, for I was busy with other plans and other people. Strange as it may seem, he has been in my mind much since I began this story. He possessed a quality so rare in men and one that means so much to the right kind of woman: the ability to love tenderly, generously, and thoughtfully. Since he was ten or more years older than I, his life may have ended many years ago, but I hope that somewhere along his journey he found a girl who was willing and able to give him the love he deserved.

During my late teens I also saw a great deal of two other young men. One was Ballard Burgher. When Ballard entered my life, he had just returned home from the Massachusetts Institute of Technology, where he had received his bachelor's degree. My family and his had been friends since Civil War days, and I have often wondered if his mother had suggested that he ask me for our first date. We liked one another well enough, but not seriously. I was nineteen at the time and as unsophisticated as it was possible to be, while Ballard, with a degree from an eastern college and four years of experience in the East, considered himself a man of the world. We had many heated discussions over my parents' refusal to allow me to go downtown to dinner alone with him. I will admit it was a rather ridiculous restriction, since the only available restaurants were the Elite, a small place that was actually a candy kitchen with a few tables added for dinner; and the Harvey Restaurant, on the second floor of the Santa Fe Railroad Station. Ballard always ended the argument with the angry question, "What under heaven do your parents think I could do to you in either one of those places, both of which are always filled with people we know?" After which he would always manage to find another couple to go with us.

A few weeks before Thanksgiving that same year, I received from Stella, my Pilot Point childhood friend, an invitation to spend some time in Austin. She was then a senior at the University of Texas and was engaged to a law student. Her fiancé, she wrote, roomed with a nice young fellow from a small town in the Panhandle, Clarendon by name. A great many pleasant events would transpire during the holiday weekend—including an important football game and a german (a dance popular at the time)—and her fiancé's friend, Bruce McClelland, would be my date for all of them.

The visit was as much fun as Stella had promised, and I enjoyed it immensely. Although Bruce proved to be a little short, a little dull, and not at all my idea of a Prince Charming, I liked him fairly well. He spoke often of his home and family, and by the time of my departure, I had learned that Clarendon was a small town on the Fort Worth and Denver Railroad and that every man who lived there, except a few shop owners and professional men, was a cattleman. Bruce's father was a surveyor with a degree from the University of Virginia. His mother also was from Virginia and was very proud of her heritage. Although she had come west as a bride, Mrs. McClelland had made a decided effort not to become integrated with her surroundings. Her social group was small, largely limited to members of the local Episcopal church.

Bruce apparently liked me a little more than I liked him. In a few weeks, he telephoned to ask if he might come to Dallas on the Saturday morning train and remain until Sunday afternoon. In those days, girls were neither as discriminating in their choice of dates nor as open in their efforts to attract the boy or man of their preference. If the man in question was socially acceptable, one was not apt to reject his visits or invitations. I have often remarked to my granddaughters that one of the numerous "bores" they date might very likely introduce them to someone really interesting.

Bruce's mother, however, had a philosophy based more on parental authority than on chance. By late spring she felt the time had come for her to meet this girl in Dallas. One day, much to my mother's and my surprise, a telephone call from the hotel announced that Mrs. McClelland was in town and would like to call that afternoon, if convenient. It was all very pleasant. We found her to be a woman of "presence," as Dickens would have expressed it, and one who must have been very beautiful in her youth. There was nothing impressive about our house or manner of life, but she evidently was not displeased. Or, perhaps, she thought she could judge me better under more intimate surroundings. In either case, within a week she wrote to tell my mother that Bruce would be home about June the first and she would be pleased to have me come to visit her for two weeks at a convenient date. I little suspected on boarding the Fort Worth and Denver train that the following weeks were destined to alter the entire course of my life.

The McClelland family, as I rather expected, lived in the largest and most impressive house in town, on the best street, which happened also to be the road to Amarillo. The house was modeled after the beautiful mansions that are preserved today as reminders of the aristocratic antebellum South. The entrance was approached from a long drive with pastures on either side. Because the Panhandle is a part of the southern tip of the Great Plains and is semiarid country, the grass on either side of the drive was brown, without any large, heavily leafed trees to form an allee.

Great preparations had been made for my coming. At one side of the yard—it could not be called a lawn—a huge platform had been built to serve as the dance floor for the large farewell party to be given a night or two before my departure.

Mrs. McClelland, as befitted the owner of the most impressive house in town, possessed the only cook in town, and she often had dinners for eight or ten with both excellent food and service. The cook was a peculiar-looking man who was always dressed in a spotless white duck suit, but never spoke and never wore shoes or socks. Possibly he was not allowed shoes to prevent his running away, for according to gossip, he was from the penitentiary and was allowed his freedom only as long as he remained where he was and pleased his temporary master, who in this case was the mistress of the house. In spite of his demonstrated talents, his bare feet never ceased to surprise me.

My visit coincided with the Fourth of July, and there was a parade in Clarendon with a route beginning at the town's entrance and extending to its exit. In the family carriage, with both horses and vehicles bedecked with paper flowers and red, white, and blue ribbons, we joined the stream of cowboys on horseback and the farm wagons filled with happy children as the parade wound its way down Main Street. In the afternoon, in a pasture on the outskirts of Clarendon, we watched an exhibition of roping and bull riding, much like the rodeo of today. All this was very new and exciting.

I spent the second week of my visit camping on a ranch. A small stream or lake must have been nearby, but I cannot imagine where, for, as I learned later, even the Salt Fork, which is a tributary of the Red River, is only a wide expanse of sand, broken by a trickling stream in the center. Only on rare occasions, as when a cloudburst hits somewhere upstream near its source, is the trickle turned into a turbulent river. I suspect that water for the camp was supplied daily from the nearest ranch camp or headquarters. Some eight or ten persons attended the party, including the couple who served as chaperones. The chaperones had one tent, the boys a second, and the girls a third.

Bruce's sister, Lila, who was a year or so older than he, commented to me that she would be without an escort for a day or so because Will Lewis was in Kansas City on business, but would join them the following day. When I finally met him, I found him to be much older, but very pleasant and beautifully mannered. Mr. Lewis was quieter than the boys in the party, and since they were always romping and running around, I was rarely with him except at mealtime. We exchanged only a few pleasantries, as he was occupied with Lila and I with Bruce.

Excellent food was served at the camp, all prepared by a

black man who had been sent with us to cook, saddle the horses, and attend to general needs. The farewell dance at the end of the stay was great fun. Several cowboys formed a violin orchestra, and the dancers waltzed and schottisched to their music until long after supper, which was served at midnight. Mr. Lewis attended with Lila, but did not dance. He spent most of the evening talking to a charming man, Senator Wadsworth from New York, who had come to Clarendon to attend to ranch business.

The train trip back to Dallas was eight hours long. As I settled down to get comfortable, I looked up and saw Mr. Lewis standing in the doorway. I smiled and waved, pointing to the empty seat beside me, saying, "What a pleasant surprise to find a companion for an otherwise lonely trip home. I must admit that I am very surprised to see you. Why would a cattleman be traveling in the direction of Dallas? The Dallasites I know are not very familiar with ranches and even less familiar with cattle raising."

He smiled and replied, "You may be correct, in spite of which I do have very important business in Dallas. This is no place to discuss anything serious, however. Luncheon is already being served in the diner. Come and join me for lunch, and after we have finished, we'll go out to the back platform where we can be alone."

As we ate, I used every opportunity to study the stranger across from me. For reasons unknown to me, I had become very curious about the man whom all of Clarendon, and particularly Lila, treated as if he were something special. He was nice looking but not handsome, with a deeply tanned and rather rugged face softened by twinkling blue eyes and a crown of light brown hair. It was difficult for me to determine his age. At the camping party, he seemed older than he did today. In the end, I decided he was close to forty, but carried his years very well. He talked easily and told me much of interest about the West Texas frontier, the unusual reasons behind his family's presence in Texas, and about the McClellands, who proved to be his family's most intimate friends.

When luncheon was over, we walked to the observation

deck. He closed the door behind us and, turning to me, said, "I'm going to Dallas to marry you, not tomorrow, not next week, but sometime in the near future. I made this decision the second time I saw you. I felt it the wiser course to tell you about this now, but don't say anything. I shall go back to Clarendon tonight to attend to the fall shipments, but I shall return after three or more weeks." To say that I was astonished does not half express it. I was so overcome with amazement that to this day I cannot remember how I reacted. For the following three hours I remained in a very questioning mood, much puzzled by all that had occurred on the trip back to Dallas. Was Mr. Lewis playing some kind of joke on me, did I react badly, would I ever know the exact meaning of the entire affair? On reaching the station, Mr. Lewis ordered a cab and took me home. He added to his good-bye at the door, "Don't forget, I shall see you again real soon."

Because of the unique nature of that afternoon with Mr. Lewis and my inability to explain any of it, I decided not to mention our exchange to my parents. My trip had been great fun, and by the time I was settled in bed for the night, I was certain of three things: first, I had no idea what it was all about; second, in all probability I would never see Mr. Lewis again; and third, I had too many plans for the summer and winter to waste time thinking about it.

4

ALTHOUGH I did not like Lila McClelland very much, I felt that the best way to show my appreciation for the delightful trip to Clarendon would be to invite her to visit Dallas for a week at the time of the annual ball given by the Idlewild Club. Ballard would get her a date for the ball and for my small dance. Lila quickly accepted the invitation.

About the first of August, 1911, I went to Oklahoma City to visit my older brother and his bride of a year, the former Alice Lane. My visit was drawing to a close when, again to my surprise, I received a short letter from Mr. Lewis inviting me to join a small house party he was planning to have on the Spur Ranch, which he had recently leased for five years. He suggested that, since the party would start in about a week, it might be well not to wait on the mail but to telegraph my answer. I readily accepted and was soon on my roundabout way to Abilene to take the train that would carry me on to Spur. I was certain the ranch owners had either laid the track or used political influence in such a way as to make it possible to reach the little town by train. The train, which made only one trip a day from Abilene to Spur and back again, was composed of one freight car and one passenger car. The passenger car was filled with farm women, each of whom had several children and a baby still small enough to be breastfed. The older children ran up and down the aisle, cried, fought, or ate gingersnaps. To this day I cannot swallow anything resembling one. I had no idea at the time how many of those wretched rides on the little Spur track lay ahead of me in the years to come.

Mr. Lewis met the train. The remainder of the party, all of

them from Clarendon, had made the trip in cars. His sister, Mrs. Chamberlain, was to act as chaperone. Her two daughters, Katherine and Harriet, and a girl named Kitty awaited us at the inn. Among the men in the party was a charming Canadian named George Pattullo, who was there to collect material for stories that later appeared in the *Saturday Evening Post,* to which he was under contract. Another guest was Bert McCardle, whose presence I never quite understood. His family had been friends of the Lewis family when the Lewises lived in Maryland. McCardle apparently had no special interest in the cattle business, but liked the ranch life and, because of Mr. Lewis's good nature, lived there for several years as a nonpaying guest, as did Pattullo.

The inn at Spur had been built by the owners of the ranch, the Swenson brothers of New York, as a necessary business addition to the little town. It was built of stucco in the Spanish style and had a pleasant lobby, a dining room, some single rooms, and one or two suites upstairs.

During the twelve-mile automobile ride out to the ranch headquarters, we crossed a wide and sandy creek without the bogging down that, according to Mr. Lewis, usually occurred. The ranch headquarters consisted of several buildings: a home for the couple who managed the headquarters and cooked for the cowboys, a large, roomy bunkhouse where the cowboys slept, and a dining room where they ate. Close by was the corral for the cowboys' numerous horses. In the rocky hill facing the headquarters, a place large enough to form a "spring house" had been excavated, and there the butter and milk were kept fresh.

The men in the house party slept and dressed in the bunkhouse with the cowboys, but the women climbed a little hill to the commodious cottage on the "flat" above. This cottage, which was kept in order and ready for use by a resident couple, belonged to the ranch's owners, who lived in New York. Every arrangement had been made for two weeks of fun. Although the resident white couple was responsible for our sleeping quarters, clothes, and indoor comforts, a black cook had been brought out from town to prepare our meals.

Since rain was not expected at that time of year, the guests ate on large wooden tables that had been placed in the shade. A dance floor was already awaiting our pleasure, and every night two cowboys appeared to furnish the music. Everyone rode horseback, talked, sang, napped, and generally had a good time.

By the time I returned home fall was approaching, and I began planning the social activities that were to be so much a part of the season. I had left the ranch with much the same feeling about my host that I had had on leaving him at the station in Dallas. He was most agreeable, and I liked him, but he was much older and lived far away. I could see little chance of our meeting often in the future. Both my time and my thoughts were occupied with ideas for Lila's entertainment, with decisions over the purchase of the necessary additions to my limited wardrobe, and with the party I was planning to have.

My father was a member of the Dallas Country Club, and the dance was scheduled to be held there. It was my wish that the dance take place a short time before the Idlewild Ball. The large new country club had not yet been built, but the comparatively small wooden structure would suffice for the one hundred fifty guests I planned to invite. I was busy making my dance list some days after making the reservation at the club when I was interrupted by a telephone call from Miss Kate, the teacher I had known at Cowart Hall. Miss Kate had not yet married the man whose wealth was to make her social position possible, and she was working as society editor for the *Dallas Morning News*. To my surprise, she was calling on what she seemed to consider serious business, and one question quickly followed another.

"Are you going to the Idlewild?" "Yes, I have had a date for several months." "With Ballard Burgher?" "Are you going to have any special guests?" "Yes, Lila McClelland, from Clarendon." "Are you going to entertain?" "Yes, with a comparatively small dance a week or so before the ball." "So you are planning to make a debut?" "No, I have never given such a thing as a formal debut a thought, but it might be fun." "Indeed it will, and I shall immediately add your name to the list."

Thus it was that by the grace of Ballard's wanting me for a date and my knowing the *Dallas Morning News*'s society editor, who happened to place much importance on the entire affair, I became one of the Idlewild debutantes of the 1911 season.

My father's response to my having a debutante ball was that it would be a pleasant experience, but he sincerely hoped I would make every effort not to be extravagant, because he simply could not afford it. Being a debutante meant formal, engraved invitations, new dresses, and numerous other expenses.

My mother, on the other hand, told me simply that it would mean much coming and going in the house and that I must remember we had only one maid, so from then on, the responsibility would lie with me for keeping the entrance hall, the small living room, and the dining room in order. I can remember dancing many a night until two o'clock and then arising early to sweep with a broom—long before the vacuum cleaner—and then wipe off everything that had been covered with the dust stirred up by the broom. Ballard was pleased when I told him of my new plans for a debut. I received the impression that sooner or later he would have made the same suggestion, had Miss Kate failed to do it.

Soon after Miss Kate's call came another surprise. I answered the telephone, only to hear the voice of Mr. Lewis saying, "I have been working very hard and I think a little vacation in Dallas might do me good. I would like to have a date tonight, but if that is not possible, could I come by this afternoon and take you for a ride?" An afternoon date for two o'clock was agreed upon. When I opened the door to greet him, I saw standing at the curb a long, beautiful black Packard complete with chauffeur. During the afternoon ride, I learned that not only had he made plans for the winter, as he had suggested on the train, but also that many of his plans had already been put into effect. He and two other young men-about-town had recently signed a lease for a house in

Highland Park. He had purchased the car and secured a cook who was capable of serving large crowds on short notice.

Although forced to return west occasionally to attend to business, Mr. Lewis spent the greater part of the time in Dallas. I refused to give him as many dates as he wanted, but nevertheless I did see him frequently.

As soon as the invitations to my dance were out, Mr. Lewis began to beg me to allow him to take me. As I have said before my parents seldom went out socially, and, as a result, neither was conscious of certain of society's little rules. I had gone out enough, however, to learn one rule: a debutante always went to her debutante ball with a member of her family. I had planned to go with my older brother, Orren, and his wife, Alice, and to lead the grand march with Orren as my escort.

I only laughed when Will first asked that he be allowed to take me. Although I knew this was not a customary procedure for a debutante, and I certainly was not in love with him, he was so persistent that I finally acquiesced. It was a mistake that put Ballard in a very embarrassing position, and I knew him well enough to realize that had he not been so well mannered, he would himself have broken the Idlewild date. In later years, it became customary for a debutante to be escorted to her debutante dance by her escort to the Idlewild Ball.

Soon after the list of debutantes was announced in the *Dallas Morning News*, Mrs. Hunter Craycroft of Oklahoma City wrote to my mother with an invitation for me. Her daughter, Love, was making her debut in Oklahoma City, as I was in Dallas, and she was inviting three Dallas debutantes to be present at Love's debut ball and remain for a two-week visit. The invitation was quickly accepted, and an invitation from my mother as quickly extended for Love to be our guest for both my debut party and the Idlewild Ball.

My dance was held in early October, a short while before the Idlewild. My party opened the debut season. In every way I attempted to follow my father's instructions that I not be extravagant. Only a few growing green palms and rosebuds decorated the living room of the Dallas Country Club. It was the Club's first official home, nothing more than a large two-story frame house on Oak Lawn Avenue. The music was furnished by a small, successful local group. Monogrammed programs announced the dances, which included cotillion figure numbers, a form of dance that was not popular for too long. A buffet supper was served at midnight.

The following morning, however, my father had a serious talk with me. He was pleased that it was a happy occasion, but warned me that if I continued in my extravagant ways, the chances were good that I would ruin the life of some worthy young man. My party, it seems, had cost the large sum of one hundred and fifty dollars. Between my dance and the Idlewild, the interim of time went quickly.

For the Idlewild Ball, Ballard followed tradition and sent me the usual long-stemmed roses with tight buds. They were neither beautiful nor easy to carry, and certainly added nothing to the appearance of the girl who carried them. The night of the ball I may have subconsciously wanted to leave them behind, for I forgot them until reminded by Ballard after we were seated in the victoria.

Because the Dallas Country Club was not of sufficient size, the 1911 Idlewild Ball was held in the beautiful new Jewish Columbian Club. The ball differed from my debutante party in every way; no expense had been spared. The ballroom was elaborately decorated to resemble the facade of an Italian villa. Special lights and an abundance of flowers gave the impression of dancing in an Italian moonlit garden. An orchestra from the East furnished the music. The program consisted of dances, waltzes, two-steps, and the Boston (a new and very popular dance).

Ten young ladies, daughters of prominent families of the city, and five visiting girls were considered the guests of honor. There were two refreshment tables, one serving cocktails for the men and one punch for the ladies. Two years later the punch table was done away with, and the women then enjoyed cocktails, if they so desired. It was also a few years later that the debutantes were presented in a very formal manner.

But on our next date, Ballard said he would not be seeing me again; that he had given it much thought, and he had decided not to make a fool of himself, or at least not to be made a fool of, particularly by a cowboy from West Texas. It made me unhappy, but there was little I could say. I was being punished for not playing the social game according to the rules.

Other occasions when I learned to play the social game were not as painful, though not always pleasant. At that time, it was customary for older women to give formal receptions every year or so and for the debutantes to be asked to receive with the hostess. My first such experience was at the house of Mrs. John William Rogers, who had once lived about a block and a half away from us. I will never forget the boring and embarrassing experience of being introduced, one after another, to two or three hundred older women, many of whom I had never seen before.

I well remember promising myself while lying in bed that night that I would not be as reserved as my mother. In time, many of the people I had met at the reception became familiar to me, and by continued effort I learned to make enough small talk to appear friendly.

5

AT the time of my debut a harmless but gossipy and widely read little magazine called *Beau Monde* was circulating in Dallas. Owned and published by a Mrs. Fitzgerald, it was a weekly newspaper that, for want of a better name, shall be described as a social or gossip paper. Where or how Mrs. Fitzgerald collected her information, no one seemed to know. Her stories in general were fabrications of a wild imagination. They were, however, always founded on enough facts to appease the more discriminating and to amuse the remainder of the public. The *Beau Monde* was read by everyone who in any way was connected with the social scene in Dallas. Already such articles as the following were beginning to appear:

> When Will Lewis leaves Spur for Dallas, the florists sit up and take notice, for then there is something doing in the flower market. Orchids and carnations, not by the dozen, but by the dozens, and where there are many dozens of them, there must be an American Beauty somewhere. And Will comes often, not too often, either for the trade or the other and greatest motive, but who is she?
>
> Did you know that there is a bachelor's paradise in Highland Park? That Langdon A. Smith, Paul Vandervelt, Ted Newsome, Will Lewis of Spur, and George Pattullo have a luxurious bungalow there? You will find it in the telephone book. These men call themselves the M.B. Now M.B. stands for many things, Millionaire Bunch, Modern Brigands, Merry Beggars, Mad Bachelors and lots of things. It was whispered that they were keeping bachelor's hall, but it was quickly discovered that they have three genuine Delmonico chefs and an Oscar menu every day, and now every evening there is a beau-

tifully appointed dinner served to a limited number. On Sunday evening, however, there are from twenty to thirty guests at the dinner table.

Ted Newsome is the first to foreswear allegiance to bachelorhood. He found Miss Marian Lane a greater attraction than the bungalow, and every one of his friends thinks he has shown taste and acumen. It is said that another one of the M.B.'s is anxious to follow Mr. Newsome's example. It was told to the Idler in strict confidence, and being a woman she repeats it under the same condition, absolute secrecy. One initial of the man's name is W. (and another is well-l-l-l, never mind, there is an L in it near the front end). They say—a dangerous informant but serviceable sometimes—that this man is fond of berries, spelled New ways and old, and our advice to him is go in and win one of the sweetest girls in Dallas. This is a Spur.

Very shortly after the Idlewild Ball, Marian Lane and I left for Oklahoma City. Marian was my sister-in-law's younger sister, and she and I had become friends during the time of her debut. The two weeks of our visit in Oklahoma were more wonderful than any other two I had ever experienced. Love Craycroft's parents lived in a large house suited to any kind of entertaining. Mr. Craycroft, as I remember him, was a big and rather jovial man and apparently one of ample means. The meals in their home were excellent and beautifully served, with one or two uniformed maids always ready to take the guests' phone calls, answer the door, press their clothes, or bring their breakfast to bed if they slept late.

Mrs. Craycroft was charming and evidently liked girls, and I quickly became quite fond of her. Unlike my mother, Mrs. Craycroft was not only beautifully trained socially but also very sophisticated. No daughter of hers would have made the mistake of going to her coming-out party with someone other than a brother or another member of her family.

A few nights after Marian and I arrived, Mr. and Mrs. Craycroft presented Love to Oklahoma society at a large cotillion in the Lee-Huckins Hotel. The men chosen to escort us to the debut ball were not youngsters but men of prominence in the business world of Oklahoma City. One was president of a bank, and the man with whom I attended all the festivities was Tom Braniff, who later founded Braniff International Airline. I grew to like Tom very much and in the years to come met often with him and his family.

The debutante ball was very lavish, and the grand march was led by Love and her brother. I returned home greatly impressed. Everything about the Craycroft's mode of life, and, as I was to learn, their approach to life, was entirely different from that of my family.

A few weeks later I again went to visit Love, this time by special invitation from a member of the club to go with him to a club ball. I soon discovered that all the Craycroft servants had been temporarily engaged for the duration of our earlier visit and that Mrs. Craycroft, in fact, ran a rather shabby establishment. I never lost my affection for her, however, and Love continued through the winter to be one of my closest friends. Another close friend, Marie Murphy, lived on Maple Avenue, and her mother, like Love's, became a great favorite of mine. I often spent the night in their home. Love stayed in Dallas as much as in Oklahoma City, dividing her time between Marie and me.

The debut winter had proved to be great fun and had also taught me much. I had plenty of dates, even without Phil and Ballard, and I still went out a great deal with my brother Orren's friends from Atlanta. Orrie Harrison was the only one of them who became serious about me.

Mr. Lewis continued to spend much of his time in Dallas, and because he had no job in town, we went for many drives in the afternoon as well as going out at night. Periodically, he asked me to marry him and I refused. Once he went so far as to bring an engagement ring with him. On that particular day we were driving along the new Mockingbird Road. Without any explanation, he turned suddenly into a short lane and drove to a clump of trees, where he stopped. He then removed the ring from his pocket, turned to me, and said, "Once again, Willie, I am asking you to marry me. It is now late in the spring, and I have been almost constantly in Dallas since fall. This happens to be a very busy time for a rancher, and I must return to Clarendon for several weeks. Before going, I hope to straighten out the undecided question between us. The debutante season is over, and you have had plenty of time to decide your feelings for me. I love you very much. Don't you love me a little? If not, I shall return to the country, go to work, and try to forget you. I can no longer continue to remain in Dallas, attempting to persuade you to made a positive decision."

At this point he put the ring on my finger. It was a very beautiful ring, but the diamond was so large it would have looked ridiculous on a hand as small as mine. Not wishing to hurt him or to show a lack of appreciation, I replied gently, "I'm sorry I haven't been able to make you understand. I like you decidedly better than any other man I've ever known. It is not you, but the idea of marriage, I reject. I simply don't want to be married to anyone now."

I returned the ring to him, and he angrily threw it into a clump of bushes some thirty feet away. After much persuasion on my part, however, he retrieved it, and we resumed our ride. He left for Clarendon the next day. I did not hear from him for several weeks and doubt that I would ever have again, had not my brother Orren run across him by chance one day on Commerce Street as Mr. Lewis walked into the Baker Hotel. I have forgotten what my brother said, but Will called me for a date that night.

It was the first of a number of dates. Will, in the same manner as during the winter, would spend a week or ten days in town, then return to the ranch to work for a few days. During this period he never once referred to marriage. I judged that he had decided on a new approach. Meanwhile, I had very slowly begun to realize that I was extremely fond of this rancher from West Texas. I suppose his absence from Dallas and the feeling that he might never return made me know how much I cared. I could not explain why or exactly when my feelings had changed, but they had.

In early August Mr. Lewis gave another house party at the Spur Ranch. This time, not his sister but my sister-in-law,

Alice, acted as chaperone. The guests were people he had learned to like in Dallas. The night before the party ended, he again asked me to marry him, and this time I said yes. He put his arms around me, drawing me close to him, and very gently kissed me, my first kiss from a man outside the family circle. He then laughingly inquired, "Don't you think the time has come for you to stop calling me Mr. Lewis?"

Because the fall is such a busy time in the cattle industry, he requested that we be married as quickly as possible, and I agreed. The wedding was set for September 19, 1912. The day after I returned home from the house party, the following inaccurate, ridiculous, but amusing article appeared in *Beau Monde*:

> Mr. Will Lewis of Spur has one of the handsomest and most delightful homes in Texas. He leases from the Swensons of New York four hundred thousand acres, which is about two Goodnight counties, and runs a millionaire's ranch. His "bungalow" is large, luxurious and beautiful. It was built by the Swensons for a son whose health was failing and who found Texas climate invigorating and health-restoring. There is installed every modern city convenience, modern bathrooms, sleeping verandas, electric fans, Persian rugs, Dresden china, Gobelin tapestries, and Italian sculptures and paintings. There is an over-abundant supply of clear sparkling water and Pittsburgh heaters and hot water pipes for winter heating. Mr. Lewis has several motor cars, any number of fine horses, and all sorts of conveyances with a regular retinue of servants to look after things.
>
> In the beautiful and luxurious home, Mr. Lewis has had for two weeks a party of twenty young people, twelve from Dallas and eight from other towns, with Mrs. Orren Newbury as chaperone. Every imaginable divertissement is offered for the guests. They take motor tours and go speeding. They ride horseback, round up cattle, and watch men brand them. They have all sorts of card games and contests, swimming matches, fetes champetres, old fashioned picnics, al fresco breakfasts, luncheons, dinners and suppers. In fact, everything you can think of, perhaps even falcon for the newest fad, falconry or "hawking."
>
> For this special—and it is rumored that it is specially spe-

cial—occasion, Mr. Lewis had built on the lawn a pavilion for dancing, and every evening the guests, if they dance, dance to the music of a magnificent victrola or an orchestra of strings. Every hour is one of delight and the guests will reluctantly leave for their homes at the end of this week after two weeks of hospitality uncommon anywhere, East, West, North or South.

N.B. Every day everybody asks everybody else, "Who is in love?" And everybody answers in unison, "Why Lew/is, of course." Congratulations, there is nothing new buried under the sun of this planet.

On the following Sunday, Will and I announced our engagement. The few weeks intervening between the ranch party and the wedding were very busy ones. Notes had to be written to the small number of friends who were to be invited. I made a hasty telephone call to Love in Oklahoma City, asking her to be a bridesmaid. Marie Murphy and Marian Newsome were also quickly notified. After much consultation, my parents and I decided that my wedding gown should be made by Carrie Waller, the most fashionable modiste in Dallas. My other clothes, however, came from a less expensive dressmaker. My traveling suit was purchased ready-made from a large store, half a block from my father's on the corner of Griffin and Elm streets—the newly established Neiman-Marcus Company. My father made arrangements with the minister for the service, and I planned the temporary flower and alter decorations. Mrs. Rucker, my former piano teacher, was asked to furnish the music. As a last preparation, I selected the silver tea service that was to be my parents' wedding gift and the pattern for the wedding flat silver, which was to be the gift from Will's parents. Will's wedding gift to me was a perfectly beautiful string of pearls.

Our wedding was very simple. The service was performed at home at six o'clock with only a comparatively small number of friends present. Love Craycroft and Marian Newsome, who herself had recently married, were matrons of honor. Dr. William Anderson, pastor of the First Presbyterian Church, read the service. After a simple buffet supper, the cutting of the wedding cake, and a change of clothes, we hurried away to catch the train for California, traveling by way of Kansas City.

I did not know why he chose that route, unless it was force of habit with Will, who often during the preceding years had transacted business there. However, I do not remember his even calling the office of his bankers, the Clay, Robinson Commission Company. During the night a hard southwestern norther had blown in, and my wardrobe for a California trip was not suited to the extreme cold that greeted us on alighting from the train. Fearful that I would catch cold, Will insisted that we go shopping for a fur coat as soon as we had registered at the Muelbach Hotel. The coat he purchased for me was beautiful and most welcome at the time, but I did not use it too much after our return. Fur coats are rarely needed in most of Texas, and because of this, I always had the feeling that they were an extreme form of ostentation.

It is well that I did not realize how ill-prepared I was for the various roles I would assume as the years moved on. During the twenty-three years since my husband's death, I have often had the awesome feeling that the young girl who lived in Dallas long ago, the woman who was Will's wife for almost half a century, and I are not one and the same, but instead a form of reincarnation. As every woman discovers, the man at whose side she lies on the morning after the wedding often bears slight resemblance to the person who courted her. Although Will, like other men, in time proved not to be the leisurely and social man-about-town he was in Dallas, he was the man with certain basic characteristics that had made me love him. He had come from more than one generation of substantial families in Maryland, so—like all well-bred Victorian men—on the first night he only kissed me and said good-night.

Both Will and I were happy together and enjoyed the honeymoon. It was all so long ago that I remember only a few brief, unrelated incidents, such as Will's being provoked when asked by a fellow train passenger where he and his daughter were going. We stayed at the famous Fairmont Hotel in Los Angeles and went to the theater to see a pleasant little comedy called *Officer 666*. We lunched at the renowned Poodle Dog Restaurant, where I had my first glass of wine.

In San Francisco, my chief desire was to see the famous Barbary Coast. The taxi driver was surprised when two obviously married people emerged from the dignified Saint Francis Hotel to make so unexpected a request. Being an experienced driver, he drove us to the only place that, on the surface at least, appeared to be respectable. It was a huge, two-story house with a large entrance hall and an equally large dining room at the right. The orchestra was playing something light when we entered the room, but immediately the music stopped, then picked up; the sudden new tune was the wedding march. The other diners simply laughed and applauded.

As soon as we were seated, I asked Will how everyone in the room happened to know we were newlyweds. He laughed and answered, "Well, to begin with, you are very young and have a look of innocence rather than one of sophistication. In any case, you do not resemble the type of woman who frequents a place like this. Besides, there may be a chance that I appear more like a contented businessman with the girl of his choice than a playboy looking for fresh game. I am a little surprised myself that prostitution, gambling, and such is allowed, even though restricted to one section of the city. I expect I should not have brought you here, and I was a little surprised at your wanting to come. However, I knew nothing would happen to you with both me and the taxi driver to take care of you."

6

On returning to Texas, we went by Dallas to see my parents and to make arrangements with the recently completed Adolphus Hotel for a suite that we would occupy during the coming months of winter. Our final destination was the Spur Ranch. We were to stop on the way, however, at Clarendon, so his family would have an opportunity to know me better. Unfortunately, none of Will's family had been able to attend the wedding. His mother and father were both very old, his sister was badly crippled, and his nieces were in Washington at school, and all were unable to make the trip.

The family was still living in the rambling story-and-a-half cottage that father Lewis had built when the old colony of Clarendon was moved from the bluffs along the Salt Fork of the Red River to the new Clarendon townsite along the approaching Fort Worth and Denver Railroad. The Lewis family consisted of Will's parents; a younger brother who lived in Washington, D.C.; a sister, Katie; her husband, Ben; and their three children. Katie and Ben's son was the youngest of the three, and my age was exactly between that of the two girls: Katherine was nine months older and Harriet nine months younger, and we quickly became close friends.

Will's father was my favorite in the family from the beginning. He was gentle, kind, and looked upon life with an understanding twinkle in his eye. His family, his duties as postmaster—a position he had held for years—and his library occupied his time. Will's mother was the matriarch, whose word and wishes were law. I always felt that because of my youth I was never fully accepted by her. I was always treated with much attention and consideration, however, for in spite of personal feelings I was the wife of the favorite child.

After a short visit with Will's family, we moved on to the Spur Ranch, which would be our more or less permanent home for the following few years. The Spur Ranch was one of the famous ranches of the early days of cattle raising, and its success story was difficult for me to accept when I first heard it (which, by the way, was not from my husband but from a college professor who wrote about it). It all began in 1877 when a young man named Hall and his two brothers were raising cattle in the hot, dry Cimarron area near Madison, New Mexico. The Halls suddenly concluded that the influx of settlers would in time make it impossible to earn a living on government-owned land, or "free grass." At this point it must be remembered that Texas was a republic before becoming a state and that through the annexation agreement, it retained ownership of all its public lands. With this in mind, J. M. Hall sold his third of the partnership to his two brothers and, accompanied by a trusted hand, set out for Texas. Remembering the ticks and fever in south Texas and the high winds and snow on the plains, he decided that the most desirable location would be under the protection of the Cap Rock of the Llano Estacado.

Hall's first herd of cattle came from Refugio and were branded with IX in 1878. He moved west and camped near Tepee City, where he planned to winter; however, a prairie fire forced him to move up the Middle Pease River, where he purchased a cabin from a buffalo hunter. In the spring of 1879, Hall purchased eight hundred heifers from his brothers, and the cattle from both the new and the old herd were rebranded with the figure ⊐⊢, which was destined to become the famous Spur brand.

In a short time, Hall moved the consolidated herd to the southern part of Dickens County, where he established the new Spur headquarters on Red Mud Creek in 1880. The following year he added the Double Block □ □ cattle to the Spur herd. After two apparently prosperous years he decided to sell his entire holdings to Stephens and Harris, who within a few weeks resold the outfit to the Espuela Cattle Company in 1883. This company continued to operate under the same name, adding the words *Limited of London* in 1885.

The Espuela syndicate added to its holdings by purchasing an additional 378 sections from the New York and Texas Land Company. At the peak of its success, Espuela owned 569,120 acres of land and 42,777 head of cattle. During their twenty-two years of ownership, the company directors must have had serious regrets over trying to operate a business about which they knew nothing, located thousands of miles away.

In 1907, the syndicate sold out to S. M. Swenson and Sons of New York, and once again the Spur Ranch was in American hands. The Swenson family probably never intended to operate a large cattle ranch, but instead to sell the land at a huge profit. Only a few years later, Will leased the land for five years and purchased the herd, which gave him ownership of the famous Spur brand—which our family still possesses.

I do not remember whether our first trip was made by car or by train. I was soon to learn that either way was a rugged ordeal. Although Will drove a comparatively new Buick, the automobile and tire manufacturing industries were in their infancy. The trip from the ranch to Clarendon, by car, required some twelve to fourteen hours of hard driving with frequent interruptions to change a blown-out tire or to fill an overheated engine with cooling water. The usual route included the creek that flowed through the ranch and, at one point, a steep climb up to the Cap Rock. Most of the creeks in the plains flow largely underground with only slight trickles of water visible, except after a heavy cloudburst. A heavy car usually would bog down midway, causing an hour or so of lost travel time. When the Cap Rock climb was approached, all of the car's occupants except the driver were forced to get out and walk to lighten the load.

We usually made the trip from Dallas to the ranch by train, which meant going to bed on the Pullman as soon as the train left the station in Dallas and arising by four in the morning in time to dress, alight, have breakfast at the hotel in Abilene, and catch the chair-car train that made the daily trip to Spur.

It had been my husband's original intention that we make our ranch home at the Spur Inn, in the little town of Spur, where good food, maid service, and companionship were available. We quickly discovered, however, that such an arrangement would necessitate being separated for much of the time. The ranch headquarters were some twelve miles out from town, on the other side of a creek that was always boggy. Since the ranch was designed as a cattle operation on which to raise a calf crop, it was necessary during roundups for the hands to reach the pasture to be worked in time to catch the mother cows before they left their calves to go to water. This often meant riding up before dawn. If we were to be together, Will and I had no choice but to live at the headquarters, using our suite at the inn only when we wished a temporary change of scenery. Will insisted that we move into the main cottage, which, of course, was his by right of lease. The house was large and most comfortably furnished and kept in perfect readiness for the owners on their very rare visits. I felt, however, that the servants might not take orders from one as young as I and one to whom, in reality, the house did not belong. Furthermore, I was not accustomed to white and foreign help. I preferred living alone, where I would have the opportunity to learn to manage and cook for a household without any unpleasantness or interference.

At last Will was persuaded we could make do with the little three-room house, if he added a bathroom with a toilet and running water. The latter was acquired by placing a cistern over the roof and keeping the cistern filled with water from a nearby tank.

I knew there were people within easy call; otherwise I would have been afraid. I did not leave the house very often because cattle were always grazing nearby, and I was terrified of the huge bulls that sometimes joined the scattered cows. I had never before seen acres and acres of flat land stretching far into the distance with nothing to break the view. The landscape was bare of trees of any kind except an occasional mesquite. From this I must have had an unconscious, mildly agoraphobic response that made me feel uneasy, as if the horizon were the end of the earth.

I have always had within myself resources that have enabled me to amuse myself easily when alone. Knowing that Will would be away from daylight till dark each day, I was prepared to draw on those resources. Also, I enjoyed being mistress of a house, so happily spent my days learning to cook, playing classical records on my Victrola, reading, or studying.

On rare occasions I cried and said I was homesick, which made my husband very angry. Because of Will's unusual personality, it never occurred to him that the isolated life of a busy rancher's wife might have an ill effect on a girl not only immature but also accustomed to a life where she was constantly surrounded by friends and parents, who treated her both as their beloved child and as a companion. For the most part, however, I was very happy during those three years on the ranch, and in his more endearing moments Will called me "Peach Blossom" and "Pollywog." I cannot imagine why such ridiculous nicknames should have come into existence, but I loved them very much.

One of my happiest memories is of going to sleep at night very close to Will; Will on his right side with my arm under his, our hands clasped, and my arm around his waist, happy, contented, and unafraid. Will also was happy and content, but was working very hard. The Spur lease was by far the largest operation he had ever undertaken. Although it had been only a part of the huge Espuela Land and Cattle Company, it still contained some 430 thousand acres, seven different pastures, and a herd of twenty thousand or more cattle.

For the smaller pastures, my husband paid ten cents an acre and for the larger ones, twelve and one-half cents. Because of the broken terrain, even the owners were not certain of the exact number of cattle remaining on the ranch. At the time of the sale an amicable agreement was reached, which proved highly profitable to my husband, for there were many more cattle in the Spur herd than either the Swenson brothers or Will had estimated. The loan for Will's purchase of the cattle was from the Clay, Robinson Commission Company of Chicago and Kansas City. Because of the magnitude of this transaction, it probably was just as well that I knew nothing about it. Will told me several times in later years that he made the nucleus of his fortune there. He realized fully that both his fortune and his dreams were at stake and that large sums of money could be made or lost, dependent entirely on his strict supervision of every detail of the ranch's business.

By the time I met Will he had the reputation of being the best rancher in the Panhandle; he knew how to manage not only cattle but also his hands. He fed them well, paid them well, housed them well, and treated them with respect. He never asked them to do any job that he could not have done himself and probably done better, if necessary. Also, if a hand worked well for him for several years, Will gave him the privilege of running ten or fifteen of his own cattle on the ranch without charge. Nevertheless, he still carried with him the social code of his Maryland upbringing. Never once did he give the impression that they were his friends, but that they were employees and he, as the owner of the ranch, was the boss.

The frontier had absolutely no permanent effect on him. He never wore a Stetson hat, which in the early days was the accepted form of cowboy headgear. He never wore cowboy boots and dispensed with the need for a boot heel by placing on his stirrup a *tapadero*, the leather hood used on all Mexican saddles. I do not remember one instance where a cowboy came to the house to talk business. They usually waited until Will arrived in town and was in his office at the bank.

One of our grandsons who, when young, spent several weeks on the ranch every summer said to me once, "Willie, you should have seen how the cowboys behaved at mealtime; they swore, they reached across in front of one another to get something, and told any kind of story that came into their minds. I remember one day when they were particularly boisterous, they suddenly heard the front door open and close. Immediately they stopped what they were doing, and by the time Papa Will had reached the table they were quietly seated, and no one spoke again until after Papa Will had finished his meal and gone out."

Keeping the windmills and fences repaired and in order was routine, but the large job of rounding up and branding the cattle began every spring about the first of April and was repeated in the fall. Will and I arrived at the beginning of the busy fall season, having just returned from our honeymoon. Extra hands had been added to the ranch's permanent outfit, and the chuckwagon, packed with ample food and the cowboys' bedrolls, was already stationed at the first pasture to be rounded. Every morning Will and I breakfasted early, and he left, either by car or on horseback, as if in anticipation of the rewards the day would produce, returning after dusk. His constant attention to the outfit's activities gave him a fairly accurate idea of both the number of calves branded and of the newly cut steers.

One night it was long past dark before he came in. Opening the door, he did not wait for me to comment on his disheveled appearance, but hastily said, "If you have ever wondered about my loving you, take a good look at me now. My horse and I had to swim over a creek almost a mile wide to get home for the night, but I was determined to come because I knew it would frighten you to be alone." He was correct. I would have been nervous and uneasy. I was embarrassed that he had made such an effort but deeply pleased that he cared that much for my feelings.

At the time I was introduced to Will, he was not at all a man of wealth; rather, he was a young, prosperous man with great potential. He was viewed by his friends and acquaintances in town (and by his business associates in Kansas City, particularly his backers) as a man well on his way up. He possessed all the necessary qualifications for success in the world of business. He had intelligence—not of the curious, searching, analytical kind, but of the sort based largely on common sense and intuition. He was of medium height and slight build, but no one ever thought of him as small. Will had excellent health, strength, and unlimited endurance. He had known from the day he witnessed his first roundup that he wanted only one thing in life—to own acres and acres of the beautiful rolling prairies that surrounded him on all sides, and the thousands of white-faced Hereford cattle that grazed them. Of most importance was my husband's unshaken confidence in this ability to achieve whatever goal he desired. I feel certain that the thought of failure never once crossed his mind. Also, he was ideally suited by nature to the kind of life he had chosen. I suspect he rarely felt the need for another person.

I was very young, knew nothing about business, and was not much interested in the management of a huge ranch. Furthermore, as I was to learn, Will never discussed his personal affairs with anyone. Later I would have enjoyed being a part of my husband's business life, but Will never outgrew his Victorian feeling that the husband alone controlled the family finances.

One evening when an intimate Clarendon friend of Will's was visiting us at Spur, their after-dinner conversation turned to reminiscences and cattle deals. The stories of their earlier days in the cattle business were delightful, but I was more interested in a recent occurrence. After our guest had retired, I asked Will to tell me more about the incident. To my surprise, he did not respond to my request, but turned to me and said, "We were discussing business. Do I give you everything you wish for? If I do, suppose you run the house and the family, when we have one, and I'll run the business."

Was this my husband speaking to me? His tone of voice was that of a loving parent rebuking a small child who continued to interrupt him. I was too bewildered by both his words and his manner to respond. I stood for a minute in perplexed silence, then turned and walked away.

It is sad that I was neither mature nor wise enough at the time to realize that Will's twenty-five or more years on a Texas ranch had somewhat isolated him from America's rapidly changing world. He had no intention of hurting me;

he was simply assuring me in his old-fashioned Victorian way that he would always take care of me. It made me wonder as to the position I occupied in my husband's life, however. Was I a partner whom he both loved and respected and who would stand by him during his failures, as well as his successes, or was I a child whom he loved and would teach and protect until the arrival of adulthood? My mind was filled with unanswered questions.

By then I knew Will well enough to be certain that he would never intentionally do anything unkind, but, nevertheless, I was both embarrassed and deeply hurt. I had suffered a wound that would never heal. During our forty-five years of married life, I never again asked about business or anything that I thought Will might consider personal, and never again did I show particular interest in anything connected with the various ranching enterprises. I simply signed the papers that were handed me and returned them without knowing what I was signing.

7

THE first summer after our marriage, Will and I stayed on the ranch except for occasional short visits to Dallas and Clarendon. During the Clarendon visits I learned from sister Katie the story of the Lewis family's move to Texas and of Will's infatuation with the plains country and with cattle and life on the range.

At this point I also began to learn certain details of Will's early life and of the forces that had played an important part in molding him into the kind of man he was when I met him for the first time. The circumstances that brought him to Clarendon arose in a roundabout way.

Will's paternal grandparents had died during his father's childhood, and, although not legally adopted, Will's father had been taken to live with a Dr. Jenks, a dentist of superior intellect and wide influence in the small town that Frederick, Maryland, was in those days.

From birth until the age of fourteen, Will lived in Frederick as the son of a typical upper-class, small-town eastern family. His mother was the daughter of an extremely well-to-do man who lived in a large and beautiful Georgian house on the old Post Oak Road to Baltimore. At one side were the slave quarters and behind, expansive farmland.

Will's becoming a cowboy and a cattleman resulted from most unusual circumstances and a series of events of little direct connection with Will at the time. His mother was one of several children of the Koogle family, the youngest of whom was Bill, for whom Will was named. It was this uncle who was destined to play an important part in Will's life. The first significant event was Bill's surreptitious departure from Gettysburg College to try his hand at buffalo hunting in Kansas. From Kansas he moved to Colorado, where he ran a freight outfit for his older brother's tannery.

While this was happening, Will was growing up and being educated at a fine private school in Frederick. His family lived in a four-story brownstone front, the first floor of which was his father's successful mercantile establishment. Behind the building were grounds of sufficient depth for a flower bed and for the children's playground. As a child, according to Katie, Will had been different from the average boy. He was always very active and was particularly interested in earning money. By the time he was six, in the afternoons he often sat on a stool in front of his father's store, offering for sale the needles, pins, thread, and buttons that he kept on a small table at his side. Because he had a friendly and not easily ruffled disposition, and was very active and good at any sort of play, all the boys liked him, but for some strange reason he never brought any of them home to spend the day.

Will's favorite pastimes were activities that did not require cooperation of another playmate. He was well liked and would swim with the neighborhood boys, but when the swim was over, he would start on some project of his own, such as climbing the trees that grew on the nearby creek or hunting for new bird eggs for his collection. Will himself often told me that during his early days in Clarendon, he spent much time riding horseback out in the country, especially to hunt turkeys for the family table. But as always he greatly preferred being alone to the companionship of the other boys.

By the time the young man was entering adolescence, his Uncle Bill had moved to Texas, where he had become a friend of Charles Goodnight, one of the owners of the famous J.A. Ranch. The fame of barbed wire as a new fencing material had recently reached Texas, and Goodnight had offered Koogle the job of fencing in the huge J.A. Ranch. While living at the J.A. headquarters, Koogle was introduced to the Texas way of raising cattle on a large scale. Since the ranch included some five hundred thousand or more acres of land, Bill was busily occupied for several years. At the conclusion of his contract, which proved highly profitable, he was a man of means, more than able to marry the girl of his choice, a beauty from a prominent family in Kansas City. Accompanied by Goodnight's brother-in-law, Leigh Dyer, and his bride, the two newly married couples left for Maryland in great style in their own private railway car.

It so happened that by this time, father Lewis had not only reached middle age but was finding that his formerly highly profitable mercantile business was beginning to suffer. Also, his health was not as good as before. The combination of business reverses and ill health placed him in a mood receptive to Bill Koogle's tale of the easy wealth to be found in Texas. It required little effort on Bill's part to persuade him to sell his home and business, join a partnership with Bill and two other men in the purchase of a "free grass" ranch in the Panhandle, and move with his family to Clarendon.

Thus, at a young age Will came with his family to the region and the way of life that was to shape him as a man. One can understand Will's involvement with ranch life only by understanding his involvement with this unusual region. The Great Plains of America encompass a wide, semiarid, more or less waterless expanse bordered on one side by the Rocky Mountains and on the other by the Mississippi River. The South Plains, which continue beyond the mountains into Texas, consist of both a stretch of tableland that is perfectly flat and of the gentler, more rolling, prairielike region that extends below the rugged descent from the High Plains and is known as the Cap Rock. It is also semiarid, where seasonal rainfall is interrupted by cyclonic storms, drought, and cloudbursts, and where running streams do not abound. The northwestern area of Texas, called the Panhandle, was unsettled, unsurveyed, and all but unknown territory when Charles Goodnight located his first herd in the Palo Duro Canyon in the late 1870s.

Here, and in parts of New Mexico, Oklahoma, and Colorado, there developed what came romantically to be known as the Cattle Kingdom. This region was characterized by a rugged life in which only the very strong survived and which, in certain ways, conditioned men so that they found it difficult to live elsewhere or in any other manner.

A "free grass" ranch consisted of a certain number of purchased acres with controlled water rights. By controlling these rights, the ranch owner also had the use of the thousands of acres of a partially unsurveyed and entirely unoccupied area that covered a strip of fifteen miles wide and fifty miles long, extending from the Prairie Dog Fork of the Red River north to the Canadian River. Rivers and running creeks in the strip were few and widely separated, but hardy cattle, especially steers, managed to find in the numerous buffalo wallows sufficient water to survive. The ranch purchased by the Lewises and Bill Koogle consisted of about thirty-five thousand acres and was known as the Half Circle K. A cattleman's ranch in this area was often bordered by a "serrated edge" with alternate sections of purchased railroad land and school land. The railroads received a certain number of acres for every mile of track and thus owned considerable land in the area. The state also held fairly large blocks of land, but purchase from the state entailed certain occupational and agricultural requirements with which a rancher could not easily comply. Nevertheless, the Half Circle K did contain one solid school block of about twenty thousand acres.

Unhappily, not one of the four partners had taken into consideration the fact that neither by experience nor by nature was any one of them prepared to manage a large cattle operation. Father Lewis, as I called Will's father, was supposed to manage the bookkeeping and other business aspects of the ranch, and Bill Koogle was to manage the ranch itself. Bill, however, proved as unreliable at ranching as he had been at pursuing an education, and, as was to be expected, the ranch failed, leaving my husband's family with nothing but the large and roomy cottage they had built in the new Clarendon.

With apparently no concern for the debt they were leaving behind, Bill Koogle left for Mexico, and the other two partners returned to Washington, D.C., to live. Out of his strong sense of honor, Will's father refused to take bankruptcy and insisted that the remaining cattle, mostly steers, be held until the best possible sale could be made. Will was probably eighteen at the time, but he had already learned a great deal about cattle raising, and because of his affection for his father and his deeply rooted sense of duty, he offered to take over the management of the ranch, which he did until it was all settled. By the time the ranch business was closed three years later, Will had become an excellent cattleman in his own right.

During his early years in the Panhandle, he followed consistently the pattern of his boyhood in Maryland, a pattern that clearly indicated a preference for work over play. He had no trouble in adapting to the new life, for he loved both the far-reaching tableland of the plains country and the more beautiful rolling prairies that lay beneath the Cap Rock. At first sight of the landscape, he must have had the sense of coming home.

Will said once that when he went to his first branding, he failed to smell the stench of burning flesh as the red-hot irons seared the animals' hides, to hear the foul language of the workers, or to see the filth and dirt of the scene. He saw only the beauty of the wide stretches of grassy land that surrounded him, the grace of the ponies as they ran or twirled on their heels when chasing a recalcitrant cow out of the herd, and the expertise with which the cow pony and its rider functioned as a team. From that instant he knew exactly what he wanted, and never once did he doubt his ability to obtain it. He knew that he would never leave Texas and that his main desire in life was to ride like a cowboy, to own acres and acres of land and thousands and thousands of cattle and horses. Fate had been very kind to him and almost by accident placed him in a situation ideally suited to his self-contained nature, his talents, and his practical mind.

My husband very successfully learned first the art of being a cowboy and later of being a ranch owner. He had purchased his first ranch, the Shoe Bar, only the year before we were married. It was comparatively small and was located in the southern part of the Panhandle, not especially good cattle country. It was, nevertheless, a major step toward the realization of his dream.

After only a few years of intimacy with the Lewis family, I came to understand how a person like my husband had been able to retain his beautiful manners and gentle ways after so many years of rough living and often rougher companionship. It was simply that he, like his parents and sister, had held himself aloof from the town of Clarendon in general. They had only a few intimate friends, all of them members of the Episcopal church. By the time I joined the family, Will's older sister, Katie, had married Ben Chamberlain, the nephew of the impresario of the Clarendon Colony, as the town was called before it was moved from the bank of the Salt Fork to its present location on the Fort Worth and Denver Railroad. Will's younger brother, Todd, who had been sent East to school, was making his permanent residence in Washington.

In the early days, many of the huge ranches in the area were owned by companies formed by English and Scottish debenture holders. In England, the oldest son always inherited all the property and the younger ones were sent away to find a new life for themselves; the second sons of the owners, therefore, were often sent to Clarendon for a few years. It was with these young men that Will formed social ties.

This environment was the basis of Will's success, but only because he happened to possess a very unusual temperament and personality. The routine of cowboy life gave him self-reliance and the ability to exist for days at a time without the presence of another human being. Such were the clay and molding processes that formed the man with whom I had chosen to live for the remainder of my life.

8

At the time of our marriage in 1912, the town of Clarendon was little more than a stop on the Fort Worth and Denver Railroad. There were possibly five or six thousand inhabitants, of whom only a few families were in any sense people of background, education, or substantial means. The day of the airplane and television had not arrived, and only the train, which came and went twice daily, brought in news of unknown places and events or faces to which the residents had not been accustomed for years. The result of this isolation was a largely ignorant and suspicious community.

Although I never came to know well a majority of the inhabitants, I was aware from the beginning of their feelings toward me. In the first place, I had the impression that they felt my husband should have married a local girl instead of a girl from the city. It was not that anyone did or said any specific thing; it was rather something that I felt in the atmosphere, and it worried me and made me a little annoyed and unhappy, particularly because I was never certain I had the approval of mother Lewis, as I called Will's mother.

As year after year passed and I watched what was happening to my husband's family, I came to view the small, isolated community of Clarendon, with its easy acceptance of the status quo, of mediocrity, and of the commonplace and its suspicion of the outsider, as a microcosm of life in its most ordinary but tragic form, where gradually generation after generation sinks into ignominy. Only the exceptional, strong character can use such an environment as a stepping-stone to growth and success.

By the second Christmas of our marriage, both Will and I

had become concerned about beginning our family. Because he was so much older than I, we had agreed we should begin our family as quickly as possible. As month after month passed without any signs of pregnancy, I suggested that I discuss the matter with our family physician, Dr. Leake. The trouble was easily diagnosed, and it was determined that pregnancy would never be possible for me without surgery.

So, early in March, I entered Dr. Leake's private hospital to have him perform a uterine suspension. The hospital was in an old frame building located on Pearl Street, not far from today's large open-air fruit and vegetable market. There was no large hospital in Dallas at the time. The first, Saint Paul's, was built by the Roman Catholics a year or so later. Heroin had recently been introduced into the United States as a very fine new means of controlling pain, but after one injection, I objected strenuously to the experience because, as I told the nurse, it made me feel as if my head had left my body and was floating around in midair. I was very ill, and Dr. Leake did not leave the hospital for several days because he was so concerned. In time, however, I recovered and was allowed to go home. As the doctor told me good-bye, he laughingly said, "Baby, I expect you back in three or four years to have me undo what I have done." Spring was beginning, and I can see as plainly as if it were yesterday how beautiful the new green leaves looked on the trees as we drove home.

The summer following my surgery, Will took me on a long and enjoyable trip. We stopped first in Chicago, where we stayed at a beautiful hotel on Michigan Avenue. After sixty years it is possibly no longer in existence, but I remember well that the main dining room had a side that looked out on Lake Michigan. Pink geraniums filled the outside window boxes, and each day we lunched by a window and watched the ships as they moved over the water, seemingly above the blooming flowers.

Naturally, while in Chicago Will contacted John Clay, the head of the commission firm through which he conducted all of his business. The banker immediately came to the hotel to be our guest for luncheon. I have often wondered what he thought of so "up and coming" a businessman as Will having recently taken for a wife a girl as shy and young as I. We had fish for luncheon and, having never seen a fish fork before, I used the dinner fork instead. I doubt that Mr. Clay noticed it because he and my husband were earnestly discussing business, but the thought still embarrasses me, and I made a decision then to add fish knives and forks to my silver chest.

Mr. Clay also sent his car and chauffeur to show us the sights of Chicago and invited us to join his wife and him for a long weekend at their summer home. Knowing that the house would be filled with other guests, all of them much older than I, I refused to go. Will was very displeased and made no attempt to hide his displeasure, but I was adamant. The car and the chauffeur were another matter. They not only gave me pleasure, but also amused me greatly. The Clay family limousine was at the summer house, so we were picked up in a small car by a fat chauffeur who wore a very handsome uniform and drove with an equally imposing manner. With his two passengers sitting in rather cramped quarters in the back seat of a small Ford, he took us on a tour of Chicago.

Our destination was Canada, but we traveled by ship over the Great Lakes, going through the locks from one to another, finally reaching the Saint Lawrence River. We spent several nights at the Ritz in Montreal, then again went on shipboard to go first to Quebec, then finally to a well-known fishing village named Tadousac. We had one most amusing experience on shipboard. Because Will had been thrown so much in his early years with aristocratic young Englishmen, he liked the English in general. Very quickly he became friendly with one of the numerous Canadian-Englishmen on board. One afternoon, as I rested in our cabin, he and his new acquaintance evidently spent the entire period of my absence in the cocktail bar. By the time I joined them for dinner, both were in an expansive and talkative mood.

By way of explaining himself to me, Will's companion said, "Your husband tells me he is a rancher ['rancher' with a very broad *a*]. Well, I know something about ranching; my sister is married to a rancher in Connecticut."

Neither Will nor I even smiled, but asked considerately, "How large is your sister's ranch?"

"Oh, very good sized," he said, "something over four hundred acres. What is the size of your ranch?"

Without stopping to consider the possible effect, Will truthfully responded, "About four hundred and thirty-seven thousand acres."

The young man looked quizzical for a minute or two, then rose unsteadily to his feet, and after bowing low to me, he said, "Madame, if you will excuse me, I think I shall skip dinner and go straight to my cabin. You see, I, too, am drunk."

Will and I liked Quebec and the once-famous Chateau Frontenac much better than Montreal and the Ritz. At dinner on the first night there we ordered fresh raspberries for dessert. They were served to us in a huge mound in the center of a dinner-size plate, accompanied by a dessert fork and spoon. When the waiter started to serve the cream and sugar, I smiled and told him that we were more accustomed to having them served in a dessert bowl, that they would be difficult to eat this way. Very seriously, he leaned over my plate and said, "This is the way the English do it—a sort of mixture of chasing the berries around the plate and pushing them into the spoon with the fork."

We were awakened that night about two o'clock by a great commotion in the square below our window. A band was playing, and the square was crowded with shouting and applauding onlookers as a company of soldiers in kilts formed and began to march. Will hastily called the hotel office and was told that England had just declared war on Germany and that it would be necessary for all foreigners to leave Canada before sundown the following day. We hastily packed and were soon on our way across the border and into home territory.

The trip so far had been delightful, and I had enjoyed it very much. Somewhere during our several weeks alone, however, I acquired a vague and indescribable feeling that the man I had married was not at all the same man as the one who had given up business for almost a year to court me, who had entertained often and lavishly with apparent enjoyment of the life he was leading in Dallas, and who sought day after day to be with me, preferably alone.

I had not yet fully recovered from the surgery in the spring and was forced to rest for an hour or so each afternoon. Will always stayed with me because he knew I did not like being left alone in strange hotels, but he was restless, and it worried me. Was it that he really did not like to travel and was doing it only because of me? Was it because he was so well and strong himself that he was unable to understand illness and its consequences? Or, and this thought frightened me, was he beginning to find the bonds of matrimony more restrictive than he had imagined? A tiny seed of uneasiness had been implanted, one that developed year by year until, after many hurts and misgivings, I came to understand fully the personality and character of the man I had accepted as my partner for the remainder of our lives.

I feared that by nature he did not really enjoy the opposite sex. He unconsciously considered women inferior both in mind and body. As a matter of fact, he did not talk to me very often, and after working all day he spent his evenings reading the *Saturday Evening Post* or other magazines of a similar nature. I do not know how much of this was due to his basic character, to the life he had lived, or to the possibility that, according to sister Katie, he had been very much in love with Mrs. McClelland's younger sister, who had rejected him to marry an older, more financially settled man.

We spent most of the fall and early winter at the ranch. The Spur lease was proving to be more successful than even Will had anticipated and was requiring all of his attention. I still had not become pregnant after several months, but I hoped the delay was nature's way of giving me time to regain my strength. Then one night, immediately after the Christmas holidays, I awakened in great pain. The only doctor lived in town, and it required several hours for him to make the trip by horse and buggy to the ranch. He arrived about four in the morning. After asking only a few questions and making a very superficial examination, he turned to Will and said, "Calm down, son, there is nothing wrong with your wife; she's going to have a baby, that's all, and because her womb has not quite yet grown accustomed to the presence of a foreign substance, it had a little spasm to show its displeasure. It won't happen again, I am certain, and in eight or so months, she will give birth to a fine boy or girl."

I remained at the ranch for several months, but Will was uneasy because the doctor was so far away. By late spring I was ready to return to my parents' home in Dallas, to await the coming of the baby.

During the two years of our marriage, much had happened to my parents. They had sold the home on Swiss Avenue, where I was married, and had built a small but well-arranged house on Gaston Avenue, within a few hundred feet of the gates to the new residential addition known as Munger Place. Their new cottage had a suite of two small bedrooms and a bath upstairs, which made pleasant and private quarters for Will and me whenever he was in town.

My stay while awaiting the birth of our baby was a very happy time for me. I spent my time making baby clothes, which would have been much prettier and less expensive had I bought them, and studying a much-touted book on the proper method of handling a baby. The author, Jackson, was what the professionals term a "behaviorist." I paid strict attention to his book and later followed every rule, much to the harm and discomfort of both the baby and myself.

Dr. Leake, who had officiated at my birth, operated on my father on the dining room table, and performed surgery on me in order to make pregnancy possible, also delivered our firstborn. I can see him now, an old but active and highly competent doctor, as he came to my bed in the new upstairs bedroom, leaned down, and said, "Don't worry, daughter, I'm here. I'll not let you feel a bit of pain." And he was true to his word. William was a large baby, and I had a long and difficult labor, but knew nothing about it.

Dr. Leake kept me under chloroform for twelve straight hours. I doubt that a patient of today would survive such an anesthesia, but he was an expert, and eventually I regained consciousness—happy, healthy, and unharmed. When I saw our son for the first time, I was much upset by his misshapen head and with a sob said to Will, "I stayed at the ranch too long. He looks like a prairie dog." In a few days, however, the head had recovered from the doctor's use of forceps, and I was able to see easily that my nightly prayers had been answered. Our son was fine and healthy and had blue eyes and light brown hair, like his father.

At some time during my pregnancy, Will had purchased a large corner lot on Swiss Avenue, the most promising street in Munger Place. After construction began, we learned that it would require at least two years in the building, and after the arrival of the baby, our quarters at my parents' house became too small. The suite in their cottage could not accommodate the trained nurse (which Will insisted on keeping with our son for the first few months), the baby, and us. Luckily, we succeeded in locating a plain but comfortably furnished home on Junius Street, almost directly behind my parents. We moved immediately, and at the same time Miss Cornelius, the nurse, moved on to a case for which she had previously been engaged.

When William was a year old, I became pregnant again. Our first daughter, Betty, was born the following May, in 1917. When she was about four days old, William became very fretful, cried a great deal, and did not toddle in and out of my room as much as had been his custom. I spoke to the doctor and nurse and was assured by both of them that there was no need to worry—he was only constipated and running a slight temperature. They were also firm in their admonitions that it would be very bad for me to get out of bed so soon after having a child.

I did not have much luck sleeping that night, since I was worried by William's constant cries. I was aroused very early the next morning by a confusion of talking in the adjoining room. There was a voice other than Will's, the doctor's, and the nurse's. Something was happening to our baby boy, and I had to know about it at once. With haste I slipped on my dressing gown and rushed into the next room. The stranger whose voice I had heard was introduced as a new pediatrician who had recently moved to Dallas. He had been called in as a specialist in children's diseases because William's symptoms, although not alarming in themselves, were continuing far too long. The two doctors agreed that there must be a more serious problem, but they did not know its exact nature.

I do not remember what immediately followed, but I am certain both Will and I were too stunned to do more than sit, wonder, and pray that our strong, fine son would have the physical strength to survive whatever was attacking him. One of the doctors stayed at William's side, and a few hours later he said, "I know what the trouble is—paralysis has set in." It was poliomyelitis or, as it was commonly called in those days, infantile paralysis.

Within a few hours the paralysis had extended all the way down his left side. In a short time, however, it began to disappear, leaving William with only a slight paralysis of his upper lip. We were told to have William ride a tricycle and to give electrical massage treatments to stimulate the muscles. The only feature that remained for a year was that he was highly nervous: had I followed my motherly instincts and rocked and coddled him for a few months, as I wanted to do, instead of following that stupid book, his recovery would have been much quicker. Still today, I grieve over my failure to give him what he needed most.

9

THE house we were building on Swiss Avenue, in Munger Place, was completed in about two years. Even now, the many memories connected with that house make me sad and a little ashamed. An excellent architectural firm had been engaged, and their architect, Hal Thompson, was instructed to build whatever kind of house I wanted. Will's personal requirements were few: first, that both the materials and the workmanship be of the finest quality; and second, that the building be constructed for permanence with steel beams and reinforced concrete. Will, with his background of strong hereditary ties, hoped that many years later a grandchild of his would occupy the family house.

I was at that time only twenty-four years old, anything but widely traveled, and for all except a few years of my life had lived in a comfortable but simple cottage. I had no idea of the kind of house Will had in mind, what the eventual size of our family would be, or the manner in which he intended for us to live. On the other hand, the architects quickly became aware that money was no object, that the husband of their new client wanted both a fine and imposing structure, and that, for once, they were more or less free to do as they wished. Before them lay a great opportunity to add to their firm's prestige. In happy ignorance, we had begun the construction of our first home.

I think I must have disliked the house from the day we moved in, for it was not a home in accord with the surroundings to which I had been accustomed. Nor was it suited to Texas or the kind of life that most Dallas people lived. We had no use for a living room large enough to accommodate a presidential reception, nor particular need for a marble entrance hall and a dining room in which the ceiling was decorated with the kind of rosette that I later saw in the palaces of Europe. As I look back on it now, I believe the house, to Will, was intended to be the first visible proof of his financial success.

It was eventually purchased by a close friend who loved it and lived in it for many years. Upon her death, the house was given to the Women's Auxiliary of the Dallas Medical Association. Beautiful weddings and debutante parties are often held there. The master bedroom was used in an opening scene of the highly popular but terrible television soap opera, "Dallas." In spite of this, I continue to neither like nor admire it. I felt much as Mark Twain's pauper must have felt when mistakenly placed on the throne as the real prince.

Shortly after we moved into our new home, my father failed in business. He was a very proud and ethical man, and his humiliation and concern over Mama and Edward hurt me deeply. I knew that Will would gladly have given him financial assistance, but neither my father nor I would have permitted that. My father refused to seek bankruptcy, for it was not in accord with his strict code of honorable procedure. Instead, he preferred to sell their new home in order to lessen the amount of debt. Within a few months the family was resettled in a very small rented house on a side street about two blocks from our new home. While all this was happening, I never heard one word of complaint or self-pity from either of my parents. Whether their silence was the result of deep religious faith or of an innate sense of dignity, I do not know.

Very shortly after closing the last store, my father, who was excellent with figures, went to work for Peat, Marwick, and Mitchell, a large accounting firm. They quickly recognized his ability and began to limit his clients to individuals or firms of wide interests, many of them in Houston and other large cities. His clients also liked him and often treated him more as a friend than as an employee.

The spring before Will and I were married, the White

Star's famous "unsinkable" ocean liner, the *Titanic*, on its maiden voyage from England to New York, struck an iceberg and sank. Among the 1,517 passengers who lost their lives was Alfred Rowe, the owner of the Rowe Ranch, where Will had first worked after the liquidation of his father's ranch, the Half Circle K. In 1917, Will became the R.O.'s new owner.

Unlike the fifty-six-thousand-acre Shoe Bar, the R.O. was a spread of about sixty-six thousand acres, situated not in the poorer country to the south of the Prairie Dog Fork of the Red River but close to the Salt Fork and under the protection of the Cap Rock, guarded from the terrific storms and cold of the High Plains. Its rolling, grassy prairies, well watered by the Salt Fork and its tributaries, offered the ideal location for cows and calves. Like the J.A. Ranch, it was one of the few early Panhandle ranches that continued operations for a long time.

It all began when Alfred Rowe, an aristocratic Englishman, arrived in the Panhandle, used scrip to purchase six thousand acres north on Skillet Creek, and built a two-room sod house as his first ranch headquarters. A little later he acquired sixty thousand adjoining acres from Carhart and Sully to add to his holdings.

Rowe ran the ranch successfully for about thirty-seven years; then Will took over until his own death. Our family continued to hold the entire ranch for the following ten years; it was then divided. Two of our girls, however, still continue to run cattle on their joint 15,000 acres.

Probably the purchase of the Rowe Ranch did more to change my marriage than did any other single factor. Without consciously admitting it, Will must have realized that he had achieved the goal for which he had worked since boyhood. From that time on he was rarely home, and I was left with the entire care of the children and the house.

It was not this responsibility that upset me, but the gradual realization that neither I nor any of our family filled his thoughts or motivated his actions—only the ranch, the ranch and its success.

Left: Willie's older brother, Orren, about 1891. *Right*: Willie at the age of four or five

Left: Willie's mother, Anna Hearn Newbury. *Right*: Willie's father, Henry Lee Newbury

Home of Willie's maternal grandparents, Mr. and Mrs. Orren A. Hearn, Pilot Point, Texas

Dallas Country Club on Oak Lawn Avenue, 1911

Left: Willie as a bride, September 19, 1912. *Right*: William Jenks Lewis, about 1911

The house decorated for Willie's wedding

Will and Willie's first home, at headquarters on the Spur Ranch

Some of the cowboys on one of Will's early ranches. Edward Lee Newbury, Willie's younger brother, is fourth from left, first row.

The house on Swiss Avenue that Will built for Willie

Willie's three oldest children, from left, Anne, William, Betty

Willie in her early fifties

Section Three

The Dallas Morning News

Section Three

Betty Lewis Is Rated No. 1 Deb of Season

Second Deb Presentation Set for Terps Ball Jan. 6

Left: Betty as the "favorite debutante." *Right*: Anne and Willie at a debut party

Left: Joan as a bride, September 14, 1946. *Right*: William, Jr., at the time of his marriage

Will in his early seventies

10

AT this point in history, Texas was still more or less isolated, far removed from the mainstream, since easy airplane travel, radio, and television were still not a part of everyday life.

The war, which had touched us closely for the first time during our last night in Quebec, was now spreading fast across Europe. Germany, by overlooking frontier boundaries and by offering its people a superb education in certain important fields such as mechanics, mathematics, and engineering, had risen into a world power.

The murder of the Austrian archduke and his wife on June 28, 1914, in Sarajevo was of little importance other than to give Germany an excuse to declare war on Serbia, which was allied to both France and England. Immediately, England and France declared war on Germany. Two years later, on its return trip to England from New York, England's beautiful passenger ship, the *Lusitania*, with many Americans aboard, was torpedoed by a German submarine. Because of the terrific explosion in the hold of the ship, it sank within thirty minutes, and most all were drowned. Although the consensus today is that the attack was the result of ammunition aboard, which gave the Germans every right to fire upon it, America sided with England and declared war on Germany.

I do not remember that the war was taken too seriously by Dallas as a whole, although many folks knew young men in the service. My elder brother, Orren, who was beyond draft age, enlisted and was sent to the so-called School of Fire in Oklahoma for officer training. All of this was commonly known as World War I, in which ten million lives, including civilian and famine victims, were lost. As millions watch on television all that is going on in Europe and the Middle East today, is it surprising that some Americans wonder if their country has yet learned its lesson?

What a year! The birth of a daughter, William's illness, the trip to Colorado Springs, a move into a new home, the purchase of a ranch, and a third pregnancy, all in the short span of twelve months. I do not know how I survived it. My father, like Will, was rarely home at that time, and during his long absences, my mother and Edward stayed with me. It was an arrangement beneficial to all of us, for that year proved to be an eventful one, possibly the most difficult one of my life.

Anne, by far the most beautiful of our children, was born in September of 1918. My health, which had suffered as a result of the three pregnancies, improved materially, and I quickly began to resume my normal life and some of the social habits to which I had become accustomed.

In the spring I planned our first social venture in our new home. I decided to have a luncheon, although I knew the cook could not handle the number of guests I planned to invite, nor had I had the time to acquire the silver and china necessary. At this time, Dallas did not have the various catering services that hostesses later came to rely on for large parties. Will and I had entertained often during the winter we spent at the Adolphus Hotel, however, and I had come to know Carraud, the maitre d'hotel, very well. So it was he who managed so successfully the catering for the luncheon. The food was sent out in very large containers on huge trucks and was both hot and delicious. Everyone enjoyed it, but I was forced to admit I was very embarrassed: as an added touch of elegance, Carraud had altered his waiters' dinner clothes. Instead of the customary black dinner uniforms, he had adorned them in short red satin pants, long black stockings, buckled black patent-leather shoes, and matching trimmed coats, all reminiscent of outfits worn during Revolutionary War days. I am sure it was the only luncheon of its kind ever given in Dallas, either in the days when it was a town of a hundred thousand or after it had reached the million mark.

The summer after Anne's first birthday, we decided to

rent a house in Clarendon and vacation there. Because the altitude is much higher than Dallas's four hundred feet, the summer weather is much like that of Colorado. We knew it would be good for the babies and easier for Will, since it was closer to the R.O. Ranch. This first stay in Clarendon, however, was not too successful. The children's nurse went with us, but the other servants refused to leave Dallas, and the only cook I was able to acquire was impossible. We returned home, agreeing not to vacation in Clarendon again until we had better accommodations.

The following summer Will leased a house in the well-known Wilshire district of Los Angeles. This time we had not only our good nurse but also a cook who was willing to accompany us. Will knew he would have to be in Texas much of the time, so, as usual, my mother and Edward went with us. The California vacation was most pleasant, but whenever my thoughts return to it, only four completely unrelated incidents remain vivid in my mind. Like all large cities, Los Angeles offered every possible kind of entertainment. There were theaters, museums, art galleries, excellent restaurants, and numerous shops and motion-picture houses, for the silent movie era was at its zenith. Will and I often walked downtown to enjoy the shop windows. One day, attracted by the display of a large jewelry establishment, we walked in and asked to see and price a set of twelve beautiful plates and tea cups with saucers, each decorated with a different flower.

When Will asked the price, the clerk said, "They are expensive, but not unusually so for this kind of merchandise. They are Coalport porcelain, from one of England's finest and oldest factories."

Of course Will purchased them for me, and today they are among my most prized possessions, not only because of their beauty but also because they were a new form of art with which I was unfamiliar. The only fine china in my childhood home was my mother's set of Haviland. Since then I have acquired much English porcelain, but my Coalport remains the most beautiful and doubtless did much to form my taste along certain lines.

For the first time I realized that my husband, although from rugged surroundings, was a man of excellent taste. In later years, when in town, he often shopped with the girls and me and never questioned the price of an item, if it was simple and fine.

The second incident occurred in our Los Angeles house. It was large and well furnished, but over the dining room table hung one of those atrocious, multicolored Damascus lamps that were then in vogue. One evening our family had been at the dinner table only a short time when Will and I noticed simultaneously that the chandelier had begun to swing from side to side over the table. Will rose hurriedly and shouted as he ran for the stairs, "Get the two children into the yard and as far from the house as possible! I'll go for the baby and the nurse. It's an earthquake!" Although not as disastrous as some previous ones in the area, it was the first of a series of minor quakes that continued for possibly two weeks and extended some distance along the Southern California coast. We sat in the front yard until the earth quieted down during that first tremor, then returned to the house. When discussing it later, I asked my mother if she had been frightened, and her reply was the most perfect description of an earthquake I had ever heard. "Of course I was frightened," she answered with much dignity. "When terra firma ceases to be firma, any sensible person is frightened."

We had planned throughout the summer to return home by way of San Francisco. Because of the number and variety of people, Will not only reserved a suite for the family but also adjoining rooms for the members of our party. Impressed by these reservations, the hotel manager called as soon as we arrived, requesting an appointment for a photographer to take a picture of me for the paper. I neither desired nor objected to being photographed, but thought it an unusual request. After a short conversation, I discovered that he thought we were nouveau riche oil millionaires and that a story on Texas and its oil would add prestige to the Saint Francis Hotel. I quickly explained that we had not struck oil, but made our living raising cattle.

The final incident was at Gump's, where, according to

friends in Texas, the most beautiful objets d'art from the Orient were available. As we walked into the store, we found ourselves surrounded by insignificant trinkets such as small decorative fans, dolls, and parasols, the kind of things that children would enjoy. Turning to Will, I said, "Either we misunderstood the name of the store, or our friend does not have the taste with which I credited her. This place looks like a Japanese store in Dallas."

"Oh," interrupted the saleswoman hastily, "I had no idea you were looking for that kind of merchandise. Please wait while I make a telephone call."

Immediately, a nice-looking older man appeared and said very courteously, "Please follow me. We have to take the elevator to go several floors above." It was then that my education in oriental art began. Many years passed before I finally reached the Orient, but from that first moment at Gump's, I felt that no other painting and sculpture had a comparable beauty. There is a fluidity of movement in Japanese art that gives an indescribable feeling of constant motion.

We purchased a pair of exquisite Chien Lung bowls and a pair of Utamaro prints. They came, as I later was able to see, from a tryptich, but in my ignorance I failed to buy all three. I had never before heard of a tryptich of Utamaro or of a form of painting known in Japan as Ukiyo-e, or figure painting. The salesman was one of the owners of Gump's and was quite knowledgeable. Before having the prints wrapped, he said, " I want to point out to you that there are a few smudges that have worn through the prints. If they were not present, the prints would not be for sale. They would be in an art museum somewhere. Even so, they are very valuable. Also, note that your two bowls are in perfect condition, even though the Chien Lung period was some three hundred years ago." Today the bowls grace my Chippendale breakfront, which also holds my Lowestoft collection and four beautiful Chinese ivory figures.

Returning home from our trip to California, Will and I agreed on two matters of importance. First, we did not want any more children. Three would keep us busy for many years to come. Second, as long as they were small, we would rather remain at home or find a comfortable place in Clarendon for the summer. A long train ride, with three babies and two servants, was an experience we did not care to repeat. Although my health was no longer a problem, and the children were no longer under three years of age, my unhappiness over the house was as great as ever, and possibly stronger, because I had come to realize that my first impression on moving in had not tempered. We were living in a mansion, but one that in no way accommodated the needs of our young family.

In contrast to my original feeling that a large family would give Will pleasure, I was soon to discover that it was not a family but only sons he wanted, sons to carry on his name and success. I still remember telling him one day that I was willing to have another baby in an attempt to give him his second son, to which he replied, "Don't go to the trouble, because when the second son arrives, he will be a girl."

Sometime during the following year or two, I forced Will to place the house on the market. I still hate the idea of a living room large enough to accommodate several hundred people, a beautiful house without a library, an upstairs sitting room so small as to be useless in a family with several children, and the absence of a large nursery in which children could freely romp and play at will. The sale of the house was, nevertheless, an unfortunate experience. I often wonder if its effect on Will was not the basis of some of his unexplained attitudes or of his shorter semidetachments from the family. Will had set out to build one of Dallas's most beautiful homes and had succeeded, only to turn around and sell it.

Because I happened to be very well organized and to instinctively know how to run the household, Will was pleased not only with the Dallas home but with my management of it. He had reached the age where, irrespective of his fondness for his family, three young children made him more or less nervous. His present business, in the same manner as that of Spur, required his constant supervision, with the result that he was seldom in Dallas for any length of time. Whether his semi-indifference toward the children arose from his unfamiliarity with them, from his age, or from something else, I do not know. Certainly, for this episode in our lives, all the blame rests with me.

I shall never understand why I did not realize what the implications, even though untrue, of selling the house would be. I am certain that many Dallasites smiled and thought, "Our young upstart from the West overstepped himself financially and is now forced to live as the remainder of Dallas lives." I am also certain that a businessman of Will's caliber would have known this and, as a result, suffered some humiliation. Neither can I understand why I was unwilling to give myself more time to learn to adjust to a new way of life, nor why I took such a firm stand without stopping to consider Will's side of the question. He was a very reserved and disciplined man, and, if I remember correctly, the subject of the house was never mentioned again. His only apparent displeasure was made clear in his manner of closing the matter. "Very well, if you are determined, I'll sell the house and move, but I shall never, as long as we live, buy or build for you another fine home."

The new home into which we settled was an ugly, two-story brick house like hundreds of other "built for sale" houses in Dallas. We lived most comfortably and contentedly there, however, just around the corner from the mansion, until all but one of our children were married. I recognized from the beginning that it lacked both beauty and style, yet I never for one moment regretted the move.

As I remember that period in our lives, I look around and am suddenly conscious of the nature of my present surroundings. Everything I see belongs in the kind of house Will built for me, and possibly my great dislike for it came from a feeling that I was not yet prepared to live in such surroundings and that my presence there appeared pretentious. My youth also may have contributed to the uneasiness I felt in running so large an establishment and staff of servants. Will, on the other hand, although he had lived a very hard and earthy life in his late boyhood, was a mature man of dignity, education, and good manners, with sufficient financial standing to feel at home anywhere.

11

By the beginning of the 1920s, our children were no longer babies. Will during this period was busy, for his success continued to grow. He was still operating his first ranch, the Shoe Bar, as well as the beautiful R.O. Ranch; besides this, he often leased much additional acreage on which he ran many cattle. Such an operation required a great number of permanent camps, many permanent cowboys, and a good foreman, as well as an owner who was not only very astute and knowledgeable about cattle raising but was constantly on the job.

I was in good health and gradually beginning to assume my place in the fast-growing city of Dallas. In general, life appeared to be going well with the family. Then, as usual, the unexpected happened. By the first of the year I found myself pregnant again. It made me most unhappy because the three little ones had only recently reached the age where a competent nurse could care for them, and I was enjoying the renewal of old friendships and activities.

Joan, our third daughter, was born in October, and, like many other stories with a sad beginning, this one was to have a happy ending. She has always been my favorite child, and by far more pleasing to me than either of the other girls.

The sad side of the story began about two weeks before the expected date of Joan's birth, when I developed a severe case of what the doctor diagnosed as dengue fever. He was worried enough over possible consequences, both to the baby and to me, to call in the fine obstetrical nurse whom we had engaged months earlier. He also hastened to notify Will, explaining that it was not the immediate danger but what might happen later that made him uneasy. Unfortunately, fall is one of the busiest seasons on the ranch, for most cattle are delivered to their purchasers at that time. So Will continued to attend to the ranch, leaving the care of his wife and an expected child to the doctor and nurse.

Will had always been a poor correspondent. He rarely wrote me letters and, as I remember, never telephoned long distance. Luckily for me, the illness did no harm except emotionally. As day after day passed and I failed to hear from my husband, I came to the natural conclusion that I was of no importance at all. I had long known that business came before anything else in his life, but I had always reassured myself that if a real danger appeared, Will would certainly make every effort to come quickly to the rescue. It would be difficult for me to describe the gradual bitterness that developed in my heart.

One night, after the nurse had been in attendance for two weeks, I remarked to her, "I am not only angry with my husband for not coming home to see about me, but I shall have a birthday soon, and evidently he does not intend to come home for that either."

The nurse arose from her chair very quietly and said, "Your birthday—when is it exactly? Tomorrow?" As I nodded yes, she left the room and returned in a few minutes, holding in her hand a large glass of castor oil. I drank it and was in labor by seven o'clock the following morning.

This labor was the most difficult of all four births. I have never understood why, because I had been unusually well during the pregnancy. I remember that it continued for hours and that the doctor refused to administer anesthetic. Finally, when my head began to draw back in the position that indicates a possible convulsion, the anesthetist, who was much younger than the obstetrician, said, "You may be the doctor in charge, but I don't intend to watch this suffering any longer. With or without your orders, I'm going to anesthetize her." He did, and about an hour later our third little daughter, Joan, was born.

Joan was five or six days old when one morning Will unexpectedly walked in. I had not allowed the doctor or the nurse to call him again. His first words were, "The baby is born, and you did not let me know?"

"You were notified when my illness began, but you never bothered even to inquire about me," I retorted. "I realized, however, that my birthday would mean nothing to you, because you have not remembered it for several years. But you were correct in one thing: when the desired second son arrived, he was a girl. Unfortunately, I have given you another daughter. I am very apologetic for this, as I am for allowing the doctor to contact you, but don't let it disturb you, for I promise that if our marriage lasts another twenty-five years, you will never again be told that something has happened that makes me need you at home."

This was a promise I kept. I had very serious surgery several times in later years. Will, of course, was always out of town, and I never allowed anyone to notify him until all was over. I thought many times since that the circumstances surrounding Joan's birth finally caused me to grow up. I gave him the few things he wanted and expected from a wife and never asked anything extra from him. It was not until after his death that I began to understand that he had remained a bachelor to the end.

Gradually, as Will's successes grew, his entire world became rolling prairies and cattle. Around him grew an impenetrable wall, and inside that wall arose the castle of self. Like a racehorse using blinders, he rushed toward his goal without being conscious of the world outside. He was not really an active participant either in my life or in the lives of the children. When they were small, he neither frolicked nor romped with them, although he was never cross with them and was always ready and willing to do for them whatever was suggested.

I have no recollection of his ever holding a baby in his arms or playing with William as most proud fathers would have done, particularly in a family with three daughters and only one son. Until William was close to adolescence, the rearing of the children, their schooling, and their training were left entirely to me. I never heard him give the children an order, or inquire about their grades or playmates at school.

Not long ago, I said to my youngest daughter, "I hope never to be unfair to your father in describing his character. What is your childhood memory of him?" And she answered quickly, "I do not remember having a father. I remember only a very nice and courteous man who came every three or four weeks to visit us for a few days. I tried very hard, but never once did I succeed in catching his attention."

As the years passed, Will continued to show more positively the basic elements of his character. I have wondered if he ever asked himself why he married me, what he liked best about me, what he did not like, and why we had not grown as close as a married couple should grow. In time, however, I came to understand that Will apparently lacked the ability to turn his thoughts inward. He could not possibly have told me the kind of man he believed he was, because he had never thought about it. It was almost as if it were impossible for him to delve deeply enough within himself to find the answers to any of my questions. He was in every way a man of action, not of thought. I may be mistaken, but I have always believed that he managed his business so well not by thought but by an intuitive process, which, in his case, never failed.

Although basically an extremely kind and generous man, my husband rarely noticed the needs of others, except for his cowboys, to whom he was especially generous. The financial assistance he provided them was good business for Will, too, but I am sure that was not the only motivating force behind his behavior. He understood the cowboys' problems perfectly, for he himself had worked his way up over that same road. He had little understanding of those whose experiences were outside of his own. Once these needs were pointed out, however, he responded quickly.

For the first two or three years after our marriage Will had continued as the lover of his courtship days, but courtship behavior is never long-lasting. In time his real self began to emerge, and, as before in his life, specific events hastened the process. The birth of our first child and the conclusion of the Spur Ranch lease had both occurred in 1915. Will and I were never again as alone and dependent upon each other until his long and final illness many years later.

In spite of these problems in our relationship, I lived a fairly contented and rewarding life. I loved being a homemaker, and the children were generally happy and well. Except for one brief period there were no financial worries, and I had both the leisure and the money to enjoy the social, club, and civic activities of Dallas. Will was bored by what was known as society, but was, nevertheless, always courteous and pleasant to my friends. Likewise, he was not interested in any of my various activities, but never complained about them or interfered.

More important than all of this, however, were my ambivalent feelings toward him. I was most unhappy over being his wife, but only once did I consider leaving him, and that for a very brief period. I never ceased to respect him and to love him in a rather unusual way. Never for one instant did I think that any of his behavior originated in a desire to injure or hurt anyone in the slightest. Will was never an unkind man. None of the things he did that hurt me so deeply and came, in time, to erode the loving and close relationship of our first few years of marriage were done intentionally. They were simply the result of his highly withdrawn personality and his determination never to allow anyone into his inner self.

I knew that as long as Will lived he would continue to obey the moral and social code of his Victorian family; that he would never be unfaithful to me; and that he would treat me with respect, in private as well as in public. Quite unconsciously on my part, I must have realized that it was I who would have to adapt and, if that were true, that I had best start to build a separate life for myself.

During the following years I became a charter member of the Dallas Woman's Club and later became president of the Dallas Shakespeare Club and the Founders Garden Club. My greatest achievement, however, was originating the Women's Council of Dallas County, which persuaded Mayor Thornton to install a crime laboratory in our city and introduce to Texas the magnificent program known as Meals on Wheels. In spite of all this, I am still not convinced that I am the kind of woman known as the typical club woman.

12

DEAR father Lewis died a short time before Joan's birth, and mother Lewis was destined to follow not long after. Although I respected both of them greatly and was particularly fond of father Lewis, I never came to know them intimately. The summers in Clarendon with the children had begun only two or three years before the Lewises' deaths, and so we had not spent a great deal of time with them during the early years of our marriage. Both of Will's nieces had been married for some time; the older one, Harriet, who had always been my favorite, contracted pneumonia during her fourth pregnancy and died suddenly. Shortly afterward, her husband was killed in an automobile accident. Poor sister Katie, who had been widowed a few years previously, was left with the care of Harriet's three small children. Like her father she was educated and loving, but she had no conception of how to train or discipline the children. More importantly, Katie was not able to impart to them through proper home atmosphere the instinctive reactions that often form the basis for the "good life." Only one of these three children found sufficient happiness in later life.

The summer that we decided to try the Clarendon experiment again, we leased a large and very comfortable house on a huge lot on the main street in town, a few blocks from Will's old family house. These summer vacation visits continued for many years, and although I did not like northwest Texas, I was quick to acknowledge the advantages for the children. The family who leased us their home preferred to live on their ranch during the summer months. There was a large barn, which enabled us to keep several gentle horses for the children to ride. Anne would have been quite a horsewoman, had she so chosen later in life, for she was unafraid and, like her father, seemed to understand the nature of the animal she rode. Will insisted that the children would never learn to ride well unless they began Indian fashion, in order to become one with the movement of the mount. I can see Will now when they were still very young, putting them astride, bareback, on a horse bridled with a hackamore. Very quickly Anne learned to ride madly around the huge lot and up and down the street in front of the house, far ahead of any of the other riders.

About this time a small group of Clarendon citizens formed a country club of sorts, some twelve or more miles out from town. The club had no clubhouse or pool, but did have a large spring-fed lake for swimming, with a stationary raft for sunning, resting, or diving; long tables for picnic suppers; and acres of land on which to romp and play. For many years, the family went regularly to the club, always accompanied by the orphaned cousins and by Fred and Mona Chamberlain, who also had children and were friends of both Will and me. The children had been taught to swim in a swimming pool when very young, and although I watched from the raft, I was never uneasy about them.

While our little family was growing from infancy into childhood, the older generation was also adding years. My mother's father had reached his eighties and died shortly after my parents moved to Gaston Avenue. There must have been a marriage agreement between Grandpa and his second wife, who was a woman of some means herself, for he left his entire estate to my mother. Although it was a small estate according to present-day standards, the inheritance enabled my parents to purchase a lot next to us and build a small but charming Dutch colonial house.

Until my father's death and my mother's last illness, my parents were always an integral part of our family life. William was their favorite grandchild, and he preferred to have breakfast with them each morning rather than eat with his sisters. The children loved their summers in Clarendon, and they still speak often of the happy vacation days of their childhood. Nevertheless, difficulties that arose from its isolation occasionally outweighed the advantages.

Our oldest daughter, Betty, celebrated her ninth birthday in Clarendon during the summer of 1926. Early one morning shortly after her birthday, I was awakened by her restless movements and whimpering. When I hastily took her temperature, I discovered it to be between 105 and 106 degrees. Will and I were terrified. There was a local doctor, but he was old and did not inspire confidence. Dallas had finally grown to the stage of specialized medicine, and the children had been under the care of a good pediatrician for several years. However, I telephoned not him but Dr. John McLaurin, the opthalmologist, who, with his wife, was one of our most intimate friends. He said quickly that Betty's only chance for recovery depended on her reaching a Dallas specialist and hospital immediately, that she should not travel without a doctor, and that he would meet the evening train with a wheelchair and an ambulance.

The following two months were so filled with one climax after another, one moment of imminent catastrophe, then of relief, that I am unable to remember details clearly. One evening, when Betty had apparently been slowly improving, her temperature suddenly rose again to a frightening 106 degrees. Will again was out of town. Both Dr. McLaurin and a urologist were called, and again Betty was rushed to the hospital. Whether either doctor at that particular moment knew the exact nature of her trouble, I do not know. I remember vividly the argument that followed at her bedside, however, with the specialist insisting that she be operated on immediately, and our friend, Dr. McLaurin, remaining adamantly against it.

Finally, Dr. McLaurin said angrily, "I will not consent to surgery, largely because you've been drinking and are in no condition to operate. Her father will be home by early morning; we shall pray to God that she lives until then. If so, we'll take the first train out for the Mayo Clinic in Rochester. Either you or I will accompany the family, preferably you, if you've sobered sufficiently."

We made the trip to Rochester, and the first thing we were told on arrival was that had the doctor operated with so much infection involved, peritonitis would have set in. And peritonitis, in those days before the discovery of penicillin, almost inevitably meant death.

Diagnosis by X ray was not yet well developed either, and a cystoscopic examination for positive identification of the trouble was required. That procedure almost proved fatal, but Betty did survive. She needed about three weeks of rest to gain sufficient strength for surgery to be performed, and it was then discovered that she had been born with a double kidney on one side. Infection had finally developed, and removal of the double kidney was necessary. The operation, fortunately, was successful, and slowly but surely she began to regain her health.

At our last conference with the surgeon before leaving for home, he wisely cautioned us about our future relationship with our daughter. "Whether she leads a normal and happy life depends not on her loss of a kidney, but on your reaction to it. Make every effort to remember that I've had numerous patients who've suffered no ill effects from having only one kidney. We all live with one heart, one bladder, and one of many of our most important organs. Her good kidney has long since compensated. She'll never think of it unless you continue to remind her. She must be allowed to live a completely normal life."

There were, however, important and long-lasting effects that even the doctor could not anticipate. After our return to Dallas, a month or more passed before Betty was strong enough to resume school activities. For once in our married life, Will remained at home with apparently small concern for business and the ranches. He was with Betty constantly, reading, playing cards or games, and responding to every implied wish or request. It was an unusual experience for me to watch. He had never been either a demonstrative or a particularly affectionate father. Undoubtedly Betty's closeness to death had made a profound impression on him, one from which he never recovered.

From the time of her illness on, Betty was the one child he was close to and to whom he talked freely about himself and his business affairs. As the years passed, she became more like her father in personality—a little more dignified and withdrawn, more self-contained, more self-confident, and less in need of human companionship. I felt that as Will grew older, Betty was the only member of the family whom he deeply loved and chose as his confidante. In time, his fondness for her began to appear to me as another form of his self-love, because of all our four children, she alone inherited his introverted and egocentric character.

In time, a feeling must have arisen within Betty, quite unconsciously, that at the end of his life her father's mantle would fall upon her shoulders and that the major decisions would be hers to make. This was probably the most important result of Betty's illness, for it not only affected her development, but, in later years, led to bitter disagreements and estrangement within the family circle.

13

In the years following, many important changes affected our family. The little girls had all finished Mrs. Taylor's School and gone on to the Hockaday School to prepare for college. William was attending the Terrell School for Boys. One summer when he was about thirteen, he was sent at my insistence to a very fine boys' camp. Each of the girls had been sent to a camp in Minnesota as soon as they were considered old enough to be away from home for a month or more, but Will preferred that William spend his summers at the ranch.

The subject of William and camp was only another of the disagreements between Will and me as to the manner in which our son should be reared. Although Will came from a highly literate family—including even the uncle who ran away from home to hunt buffalo in Kansas—Will placed little importance on education, probably because he had been forced to leave school at an early age and had found his loss to be no detriment to financial success.

From the beginning, my husband and I had differed widely in our approach to our son. Will seemed to feel that a son had been given to him for only one purpose—to become a well-trained cattleman, rancher, and businessman, capable of handling the small empire Will intended to leave when his life ended. I was strongly opposed to the idea, for what I considered very logical reasons: William was not at all like his father, either in temperament or in physical strength, as his comparatively early death from cancer later proved. He was far more like me—a good student, intellectually curious, a little shy, and more sensitive to people and life in general. I had other reasons, however, that were less objective. I felt it inadvisable for a boy like William to work for a man as successful and overly confident as his father. From early boyhood our son was sent to the ranch to spend his vacations surrounded by tough, rough, and illiterate cowboys. In every possible way, his father had attempted to instill in him the idea that city dwelling was effeminate and that virility came from hard work and out-of-doors living.

Possibly the angriest exchange that ever passed between Will and me took place one summer when William was about fifteen. Like all the other families in Clarendon, we had gone on the Fourth of July to watch the numerous cowboys race, rope cattle, and do the many things that are performed in today's rodeos. Because I was not particularly interested in the arts of the cowboy, I had paid little attention to the program. Suddenly I heard the words "the bull riding event," and out from the pen, on top of a wild bull, came our son. I was infuriated. I turned to Will and said, "Possibly now I can make you understand why I loathe this part of the world so much. To think of having our only son reared in an atmosphere where the standards of manhood and bravery are based on willingness to risk being gored to death, or to be maimed for life from a fall and the trampling of an infuriated bull, is all beyond my comprehension. Take me home—I'll leave this kind of sport to the natives."

Luckily William was not seriously injured, and he never again chose to ride a bull. Although the bull-riding episode occurred two or three years after our disagreement over summer camp, Will was fully aware of my feelings about William's training as a cowboy, and I believe that Will had agreed to the camp as a minor concession to me, a concession that would have no permanent effect on his long-range plans.

When William left for camp, I told him that he was to go each summer until he learned to participate in every sport that was offered. Poor boy. He made every effort because he hoped never to be forced to return to Minnesota. When he returned home, he brought with him a beautiful silver vase engraved in large letters.

The Endeavor Cup

To William J. Lewis for his continued but unsuccessful effort to master the various sports offered at camp.

The damage was done, and my husband had won. From that period on, I made no effort to redirect our son's life. I did later succeed in having him attend the University of Texas for one year. He made excellent grades, but was most unhappy, and I offered no resistance the next fall when Will said simply, "He's not going away to school again. He's needed on the ranch, and that's where he belongs and will remain from now on."

During this period, the girls were growing up rapidly. Betty remained well and strong and was preparing to attend college in the East after finishing at Hockaday. Will felt about all this special education for the girls exactly as he had about William, but with one great difference: they were not needed at the ranch, and if this foolishness, as he considered it, meant so much to me, he would offer no objection.

Although these were years of growing differences between us, Will and I sometimes went out socially when he was not at the ranch. Society in Dallas was still somewhat divided but not, as previously, into the church and the social sets. Rather, it had formed into groups that favored either the Hesitation Club or the Idlewild Club. Will had become a member of the latter a few years after our marriage. It is unwise to give a blanket description of any group, but broadly speaking, the Hesitation Club might be considered the forerunner of today's jet set, while the Idlewild members came from the more conservative group of business, professional, and family men, whose ideas and ideals formed the foundation of the Dallas of today.

Because Dallas was then still a comparatively small city, the older crowd always included the younger couples when they entertained. There were many large luncheons at the Woman's Club, and small seated teas at home for eight or ten were popular. To everyone's delight, the large afternoon reception was on its way out, and most large night parties were dinner dances at the Dallas Country Club, which was no longer the small wooden structure where I had given my debut dance, but a large, modern brick clubhouse.

Unlike my husband, I found it all very pleasant. I enjoyed people and loved to dance. Unfortunately, I have only one vivid and lasting memory of those days—that of my dignified and antisocial husband. I can see him now, not sitting, but standing against the wall, just standing, not talking to anyone, as I danced happily by. The memory makes me very sad. I failed to act upon the fact, of which I was very conscious, that he disliked any kind of social gathering and that he had decided that, since he had nothing in common with the majority of my Dallas friends, he would not bother to be entertaining or entertained.

I also felt that my husband had little understanding of me. He said to me more than once, "You are one person who will never feel the need for a drink. People must stimulate you in the same manner that liquor stimulates others. Whenever you are involved with friends, you act exactly as if you have had a drink or two."

Will also failed to understand that my behavior was characteristic of that of the social set to which we belonged. Everyone talked easily and openly to one another, called each other by first name, and never felt a great need for dignity except on special occasions. I regret that I was not a more understanding wife, for it all must have made him uneasy, at the very least.

After we had been married about twenty years, Will turned to me one evening as we prepared for bed and said, "I've made a decision tonight that I hope won't affect your life too much. I do not care how much you go out socially, and I know you have many friends who'll be pleased to take you with them. I hate this kind of thing, and I shall never again act as your escort."

I knew him well enough to know that the decision was final, so I accepted it without argument. For the following two or three months, I continued to engage in my former activities. One friend of mine disliked my husband very much and was always eager to have me accompany them. I gradually began to realize, however, that in an indescribable way, some of the men's attitudes toward me were slightly different. In our crowd were several most attractive men, all fairly close to my age and fair game, had I wished to play that way. But I did not. During the following years, I rarely went out in the evening until the fall Betty made her debut.

14

IN 1924, Andy Pondrom, who had been my father's intimate friend in Pilot Point and who had moved to Dallas with him, became president of the prestigious City National Bank. One of his first steps in that position was to offer my father the position of comptroller at the bank, a position that not only did much to erase the memory of his business failure, but also enabled him, in his own right, to be at ease and live without a financial worry. Although the position was not comparable to the positions of the higher officers, Father was nevertheless an officer and was very proud.

Meanwhile, many important changes were transforming America. When Herbert Hoover became the new president in 1929, he inherited the political result of the Teapot Dome scandal and of an agricultural depression, the effects of Prohibition, and the jazz age. Hoover continued to hold the confidence of the people, however, which was largely inspired by his performance as secretary of commerce in the two preceding administrations. The unemployment rate and taxes were both comparatively low, stock prices were rising sharply, and corporation profits were high. The debt that resulted from World War I had been reduced to $16 billion, and the fiscal year of 1929 saw a surplus of $735 million. Only the most pessimistic economists saw any financial trouble ahead. All over the United States there was a frenzy of speculating both on margins and on borrowed money—a frenzy that included not only shoeshine boys, window washers, maids, chauffeurs, barbers, clerks, and secretaries, but also doctors, lawyers, dentists, nurses, and other professionals. By September, the economy of the Hoover administration had become extremely erratic.

In the words of Dr. Arthur A. Smith, retired economist for the First National Bank in Dallas: "The crash was in the stock market where prices had risen sensationally over the previous eighteen months or so, to record highs far beyond any sound relationship to underlying real values. The boom reached its peak in September, and the first warning of trouble came on Thursday, October 24, to be followed on Tuesday, October 29, by the worst crash in stock market history. Approximately five thousand banks failed, over one-fourth of the labor force was out of work, and numerous suicides occurred during the next forty months."

Television had not yet been invented, and instant communication with the outside world was not yet present in the average household. Our ranch affairs were in excellent condition, and my small social group paid slight heed to the suffering of the millions outside Texas and gave little thought to the probable long-range effects of the crash on us.

On December 31, 1929, the City National Bank, where my father was so happily employed, merged with the American Exchange Bank of Dallas to become the First National Bank. Like the stock-market crash, which preceded the merger by two months, it had no visible effects on our family at first. As I look backward, however, it looms as the ominous beginning of the most difficult, and sometimes saddest, fifteen years of my life; years that, together with much happiness and achievement, also brought death, war, and the severest drought in the history of the Great Plains.

A short time after the bank merger, my father found on his desk without warning one day a note giving him two weeks' notice. The note was brief, to the point, and without explanation. It was the manner of the dismissal, as much as the severance of his connection with the bank, that wounded him so deeply. None of the family was ever able to make him understand that his dismissal was a result of a turnover among most of the officers. Since my father was very close to retirement age, it was only wise for the board to choose the comptroller from the American Exchange and hire a much younger man. Not Andy Pondrom but someone else was then made president of the newly formed bank. The cult of the worship of youth was showing the first signs of life, and we all knew that my father would never again be one of any working force. As I had during other crises, I watched and suffered with him as he lived through one of life's great tragedies: that of an older human being whose physical and mental conditions are excellent, being forced to sit on the sidelines of life, awaiting the end.

My father's unfortunate experience with bankers was destined to be followed by Will's own experience. The very important difference was that my father's was between banker and employee, and my husband's was between banker and customer, and in the end Will was able to avert the feared catastrophe. Although Will had never ceased to continue a close connection with the Clay, Robinson Commission Company in Kansas City, he had for many years followed the policy of borrowing his operating capital from a local bank, the Donley County State Bank of Clarendon. I have never understood the businessman's theory that it is more profitable to operate on borrowed money than on one's own. I had known Will on several occasions to borrow money when he had one or two hundred thousand dollars lying idle in the bank. In any case, his policy with the Clarendon bank had been in operation so long that he never gave a thought to any potential difficulty in renewing a loan or to the possibility of the bank's selling his note.

One night in the spring of 1934, Will arrived home from the ranch both unexpectedly and late. As soon as the children were in bed, he closed our bedroom door and said, "I'm going to fail. Everything I've worked for all these years will be lost."

With this statement he began to cry. It was the only time in our long marriage that I ever saw him shed a tear. Then he continued, "When I walked into the bank yesterday to discuss business, I was met with the startling announcement that the bank no longer held my note. The recession that's general throughout the country had made it necessary for them to get cash in the only way they knew. My loan was the bank's largest, so they disposed of that first. I know the banker in Kansas City to whom it has been sold, and his primary purpose is for me not to pay but for him to collect the collateral, the R.O. Ranch. I'm unable to stop him. The recession has hurt me too."

It was a moving experience to see a strong, self-confident, and successful man so humbled, and I waited a few minutes before answering. At this point, it must be remembered that I had been reared in a strict Presbyterian family, whose marriage vows were not taken lightly. I had married "for better or for worse." I had enjoyed the "better" days; I would now have the opportunity to prove my worth during the "worse" days. Naturally, on stressful occasions such as this, one does not stop to reason—one acts instinctively. Without any attempt to be noble or otherwise, I answered Will in the manner I had been taught that any good wife should. "Let me say to you that I don't believe you are going to fail—as good a businessman as you, and one with your reputation, will find a way out. It will take work and sacrifice, but we'll all work with you. Don't forget that we all believe there is no finer cattleman anywhere. If you don't succeed, I can think of no one else who will."

We talked long into the night about the things that must be done. I suggested two people from whom the money might be borrowed: the first was the wealthy husband of my former schoolteacher, Miss Kate, but Will's answer to that was that her husband was exactly the same kind of banker as the Kansas City banker who had the loan. The loan was due in a very few weeks.

Next I suggested George Pattullo, who had been best man at our wedding and a nonpaying guest at the Spur Ranch for many years. Pat, as we called him, had long since given up writing, had married the very wealthy daughter of a retired cattleman (who had probably started as a trail driver), and had moved to New York to live the life of the idle rich. His reply to Will's request for a loan was prompt. He had plenty of money and would be delighted to make the loan at 12-½ percent interest, at that time a ridiculously high figure. I don't remember whether Will even responded to the wire.

The first week or ten days of the period before the note was due passed quickly. Every possible source of obtaining a new loan had been contacted without success. Will was very depressed, but foreclosure was not to be part of his life plan; his reputation as an honorable and thoroughly dependable businessman was to bring its just reward. One morning a telegram arrived from a rancher-banker in Kansas named John Huddleston. He had not really been what Will would have considered a friend—merely a landowner to whom Will for many years had shipped his steer crop each summer to be fattened before delivery to the market in the fall. The telegram was brief but to the point. "Have recently heard from the Clay, Robinson Company of your predicament. Have no intention of allowing some slick Kansas City banker to take away the ranch belonging to a fellow like you. Wire me the sum you need." In this usual Cattle Kingdom manner, the note was paid, and the beautiful R.O. Ranch remained in Will's hands.

Whether such simple methods of contracting for a large sum of money were accepted in the general business world, I doubt. I do know, however, that they were customary in the Cattle Kingdom. I remember having often seen Will and a prospective buyer sitting on a fence rail at a roundup, making arrangements for the sale and delivery of Will's calf crop some several months later in the summer. After the usual handshake that closed the deal, each man would write the necessary information in pencil in the little red notebook that all cattlemen carried in their shirt pockets.

Just before the loan crisis the first signs of other difficulties had appeared. The rains of the summer and fall seasons in 1933 had not been as abundant as usual. The drought was not severe enough in the beginning, however, to be of much concern either to Will or to the other cattlemen of the Great Plains. William had graduated from the Terrell School in June and had entered the University of Texas before Will discovered the sale of his note. I shall never understand why he did not force a cancellation of the enrollment, since both he and William himself were opposed to William's entering college. William was very unhappy at the university and was most eager to assume his job as a regular cowboy on the ranch at thirty-five dollars a month. Being an apprentice to his father, however, was not going to be easy.

Outwardly, William remained toward me a dutiful and respectful son, but he apparently never forgave me for my attempt to make something other than a cattle raiser of him, and I never felt that I was anything but right. His fine mind and great consideration for others could have done wider good in another field, and I think he himself would have felt a greater sense of accomplishment than merely continuing in his father's success. After he returned to the ranch to live with the other cowboys, I rarely saw him.

William made his final commitment to ranch life just as the drought worsened. Each succeeding year without rain, the grass became poorer and more lacking in nutriment, and the cattle were beginning to die. Very quickly portions of the Texas Panhandle joined Oklahoma in becoming part of the Great Dust Bowl, so magnificently described in John Steinbeck's *The Grapes of Wrath*. Some relief came to the cattlemen from a government program that subsidized the destruction of a major portion of each herd.

During these years Will was so hard-pressed for cash that he assembled his outfit and gave them the option of leaving or continuing to work without pay until conditions improved. Most of them remained, largely from loyalty but partly because jobs were scarce, and a place to sleep and board were assured on the ranch.

At home, I fired all the servants but dear, good Maude, who had been with us for years and who I knew would stand by us through any crisis. Because today's labor-saving devices were not yet available, she was forced to spend much of her time in the laundry washing and ironing, in order to keep the three girls neatly dressed at school. She cooked whenever she could, and at other times I cooked and cleaned house with the help of a half-drunk black man whom no one else would hire. Despite his inadequacies he was kind and faithful, and I would not have made it through the difficult years without him. I attempted to economize in every way possible, bought no clothes, and limited my social life to my two clubs. It was all very difficult, for the girls were growing up, and Betty was already registered at Vassar, to enter in the fall of 1934. I felt it essential that she graduate from Hockaday as planned. I remember well going to Hockaday to tell them I would have to pay the tuition monthly rather than ahead, as was customary, and leaving behind as security a beautiful amethyst necklace and earrings that Will had given me.

Never once in the later years of our marriage did Will tell me he appreciated my confidence in him and my willingness to help him work through his financial difficulties. He simply accepted it, I suppose, as the kind of duty that was expected of a wife.

One evening in August, while we were still in Clarendon, Will looked up from his paper and without preamble or apology said to me, "It's not necessary for you to return to Dallas early, because I am not going to send Betty to Vassar. It is true that I'm no longer facing immediate foreclosure, but the cattle business is not good because of the drought, and the loan from a friend must be paid off quickly. To do this, we must be careful to spend money only on that which is important, and I don't consider college important, particularly for a girl."

I must have realized that this might happen, for I was not too surprised. I remained quiet for a moment and then slowly answered, "I'll not argue with you. The differences in our attitudes toward life have been apparent to me for a long time. We live in two entirely different worlds. When I discovered that William's college career was to consist of one year at the university, I, like you, came to a decision. Our marriage is no longer of importance to either one of us. Certainly, if remaining as your wife doesn't get for me the things I want for my girls, I'll give this farce up and divorce you."

"For God's sake, don't do that," Will remonstrated. "Such a move would certainly 'break' me now."

That was the only time in our long life together that I threatened to leave him. I had no idea whether I would or would not have carried out the threat. Will must have been certain that I would. The subject of educating the girls was never discussed again. The check to Vassar was mailed without protest, but, by way of assistance, I placed Anne and Joan in public school. I also went to talk to the principal on the day they registered, for I was particularly concerned about Anne, who was scheduled to take her first college board examinations the following June. I shall never forget his reply to my request that they take certain subjects in order to prepare for college.

"You don't understand the public school system, Mrs. Lewis. We don't attempt either to educate or to prepare for college the masses with whom we're forced to work. We attempt only to give them a smattering of a majority of subjects. The ones who are not too bright will, in this way, at least be introduced to various phases of life. The intelligent ones will discover that they have to go further to be really educated, and, like your girls, they'll go on to college."

I often think back on his remarks when I hear of, or read, complaints about America's poor educational system. If this particular principal's idea was the general idea of all principals, it is easy to understand why the public school system is in the condition it is in today.

15

For some time I had been considering writing down for the children the wonderful stories I had heard from various sources of their father's early years on the western frontier and the specific circumstances that had molded him into a professional cowboy.

In the beginning, I had no idea of accomplishing anything more than an amateurish effort to record interesting stories of the early years in the Panhandle, stories a professional writer would have had no opportunity to collect, and especially not from Will. I never quite understood my husband's ability to tell his tales so well, because he was a man of few words. I learned early that he did not talk well if others were present, or if I requested that he repeat something he had described in detail only a night or two before. Although he was anything but gregarious, my husband did enjoy the company of two men in Clarendon with whom he had worked as a cowboy. One, like Will, owned a large ranch, and the other was president of one of the two Clarendon banks. They often came to our house for an evening of reminiscing, and the tales they told were wonderful. I soon learned to sit quietly as they talked and to listen without interrupting. The following day I would write as accurately as I could from memory. Later, I realized that no reader would be able to understand the various incidents without some knowledge of the unusual nature of the land and the manner in which it came to be settled. The account that I envisioned would require a great deal of both study and hard work on my part.

One evening when Will and I were in the country alone, I asked which one of his friends would be best suited to tell me about Clarendon and the Panhandle frontier during the early years when Will and his parents were new arrivals. He smiled and answered quickly, "Almost anybody I know, but the best source probably would be your good friend Kate McClelland, whom you were visiting when we first met."

Since I had never conducted an interview, on my return to Dallas I contacted my friend Dr. Herbert Gambrell, a professor of history at Southern Methodist University, who furnished me with explicit directions. Before beginning the interviews I spent many hours at the Panhandle-Plains Historical Museum at Canyon, reading and copying much valuable information. I was always accompanied by my close friend Mona Chamberlain and Mona's son, Kelly, who was pleased to act as chauffeur. We then began the long and tedious job of interviewing the many people on my suggested list.

One evening when Will and I were alone and I was especially busy on my notes, he looked up from his copy of either the *Saturday Evening Post* or the *Cattleman* to inquire about what I was working on so earnestly. I answered a little apologetically that I was trying to write a book. "Writing a book?" he queried after a moment. "Don't I give you all the money you want? Don't you like the children? Don't you like being my wife? If you do, why in heaven's name do you find it necessary to write a book?"

My reply was a simple "I don't know." My husband had posed a question that over the years I have often been asked —a question I am still as unable to answer as I was then.

On one of my numerous trips to the museum in Canyon, I had been fortunate enough to meet Dr. Lester Fields Sheffy, a professor at West Texas State University in Canyon, who was an authority on the subject of Old Mobeetie, a frontier trading post. He was interested enough in my project to ask me to send a few of my sketches to him for criticism and suggestions.

One evening on the way home from Canyon, our driver stopped the car and said, "Please take time to look at what is ahead of us." For a distance of some twenty or thirty feet there extended from one side of the road to the other a solid mass of tarantulas. It was a frightening and sickening sight, and to this day I have never discovered a satisfactory explanation of what I saw. A week or so later, when I packaged a few sketches to mail to Dr. Sheffy, I included my recently written story on the tarantulas. My sketches were quickly returned to me with a letter from the professor saying that instead of examining them himself, he had given them to his senior class students with directions for criticism. Each story had comments written at the bottom, but only one made an impression because it taught me a lesson I never forgot. At the end of the tarantula story was the following note: "If Mrs. Lewis plans to write about the Panhandle's birds, animals, and insects, I suggest that she learn something about their habits. Tarantulas do not crawl out from under rocks, but burrow into the sand."

By the time I contacted the last old-timer, I had in my possession forty-two interviews, an accomplishment that had required endless driving from one end of the plains to the other. Much driving was done when the Dust Bowl was at its most severe, and Mona and I encountered many storms. Only those who have experienced them will accept with credence another's description. Often, while driving down the highway, something resembling a dark cloud would suddenly appear ahead of us, and almost instantly we would be in darkness. It was impossible to see beyond a few feet. There was nothing to do but drive off the highway as far as possible onto the grass, or into a gully at the side. These were frightening experiences, but there were few accidents, since other drivers were of necessity as cautious as we.

How much time was required to gather all this information I do not remember, but at last the manuscript was finished and ready for typing. I have always had the feeling that the book was not planned, organized, and written, but, in a manner of speaking, evolved itself. About this time I asked Will if he knew a good typist, and he answered, "No, but I'll find one for you. However, before you give all you have written to her, I hope you'll remember how inclined you are to ramble on once you've started. My chief concern is to prevent your telling some foolish story that could cost me one of my ranches."

The only available typist was in a town some twenty miles from Clarendon, and we drove over to pick up the manuscript in one of the worst rain and electrical storms I have ever encountered. That was only the beginning of the many problems involving my first experience with publishing. To acquire an agent is quite as difficult for the author of a first book as to acquire a publisher. In desperation I finally signed a contract with two men, one a Clarendon printer and the other the editor of the *Amarillo Globe News*, to become my publishers. The book was to sell for $2.75 and I was to receive a royalty of $0.50 a copy.

It was very exciting for me when I received the printer's first finished copy, but my momentary pleasure was quickly dispelled by the realization that misprints and other mistakes were so numerous that correcting them would be an impossible task. Will was at home at the time, and on seeing my distress quickly asked what had gone wrong. I told him that I had been caught in a most embarrassing position: since I had signed an agreement, I had no legal way of preventing the publishers from binding and selling the copies the printer had recently finished; but I should always be both embarrassed and ashamed at having a book under my name filled with mistakes and misprints.

Will said quietly, "Don't worry over it. I'll have it straightened out very shortly." What he did was to call McCarty, the editor of the *Amarillo Globe News*, and tell him the printing had been done so wretchedly that he could not allow it to be published. Will insisted that a new and dependable printing firm must be found, and that out of respect for his wife, he was willing to bear the cost only on the condition that the original printer agree to destroy the thousand faulty copies.

Finally, the newly printed copy reached me. The paper was not fine, but the book itself was most appropriately bound, and I was delighted. Because the thousand copies were quickly sold, I did not understand why a second printing had not been ordered until a series of events began to come to my attention. First, my husband learned from the president of the bank that the Clarendon Press, or original printer's, note for the faulty first printing was as yet unpaid. Knowing that the Clarendon partner was only a printer without substantial assets of any kind, Will hastened to contact McCarty in Amarillo. To his surprise he learned that McCarty had been dismissed from his position as editor of the *Amarillo Globe News* and was himself in financial distress. Without further ado Will paid the note.

I was both embarrassed and hurt that in the end it was, to some extent, Will's money as well as my efforts that had achieved the goal that meant so much to me. A few years later I discovered that the faulty copies had not been destroyed, but were currently being sold in paperback form all over the Panhandle. When I related to Will that I wished to take legal steps against the two men, since they had both failed to live up to their agreement with me and had only sent one small royalty payment, he firmly replied, "No indeed, you're not going to bring any kind of steps against the men. I will not allow it. They are both suffering from hard-pressed financial reverses, and you certainly do not need the money. You had the pleasure of writing the book and seeing it published, and that is all that is necessary."

Will lived for some twenty years after the incident, but when he died he had never once opened the book to read a line or look at the pictures. I continued to be unable to understand the character of a man who so willingly drove me through rain and lightning to pick up the manuscript, spent almost one thousand dollars to have a corrected copy printed, and paid off a good-sized bank note of the publishers, but who remained firm in his disapproval of the project, which in the beginning had been mine alone.

16

THE drought had affected mainly the High Plains area that extended from Amarillo through Oklahoma, New Mexico, and Kansas. It greatly compounded Will's financial difficulties during 1933 and 1934, forcing him to buy an excessive amount of feed and to postpone repayment of the Kansas friend who had prevented the loss of the R.O. Ranch. Although the severe drought on the High Plains continued for several more years, creating the desolate Dust Bowl, abundant rain fell in 1935 on the ranches below the Cap Rock, and with the moisture came green pastures and a return to prosperity. We were quickly able to restaff our household and resume our customary way of life.

Anne and Joan had been reinstated in Hockaday after only one year in public school. By 1935 Joan had entered high school and Anne was in her final year. Even before Anne took her final college boards, I had come to realize that Vassar would be impossible for her without another year of preparation, and arrangements were made to send her to Holton Arms, in Washington, D.C.

As soon as Anne had finished her college boards, she and Betty took an all-night "sleeper" plane to New York. From there they went by ship on their first trip to Europe. Since the memory of Will's late financial ills was still fresh, it was an inexpensive and makeshift tour, not the fine one I had so long planned for them.

As Anne and Betty came back through New York, they went out to Bronxville to see Sarah Lawrence Junior College, and it was then that Anne decided she wanted to go there rather than to Vassar. After attending Holton Arms for a year, she entered Sarah Lawrence in the fall of 1937. It was an ideal school because it revealed to Anne not the practical but the more beautiful and refined elements of life, such as music, art, literature, and the theater.

When Betty graduated in June of 1938, Will and I went east. I doubt that I had ever previously been, or shall again be, as proud as I was on the morning when we watched Betty, all dressed in cap and gown, walk down the aisle to receive her diploma. As a psychology major, she had been assisted by the school in securing a job in the New York State School for Wayward Girls. For once I did not have to make a serious decision, for Will's response was a quick and decisive no. Betty did not care to argue, since it was obvious that that was his final word, and she was soon on her way home to assume the role in life that her father considered proper for her. The next fall she made her debut at the Idlewild Ball.

During the many years since my debut, the Idlewild Club had changed considerably. Becoming a debutante was no longer a simple choice made by the girl and her family; the choice was made by the club itself. During the summer Betty's father and I received a note from the president of the club asking permission to call, and Betty received an engraved card that read:

THE IDLEWILD CLUB
Extends an invitation to
Miss Betty Lewis
to be presented at its
Fifty-fifth Annual Ball
Friday evening, the eleventh of November
One Thousand Nine Hundred and Thirty-eight
at ten o'clock
The Baker Hotel
Dallas, Texas

When the invitation was formally accepted, Betty was told that her escort would be Robert Perry, one of the club's officers. We were soon busily planning Betty's debut parties and shopping for the various clothes necessary for so busy a social season. At Neiman-Marcus one day, as Betty and I had just finished selecting the ball gown we preferred, Mr. Marcus himself (not Stanley, but his father) entered the fitting room. He agreed that the gown suited her beautifully. On learning the price, however, I remarked that we still had not completely recovered from the drought and that I thought it unnecessary for anyone as young as my daughter to spend so large a sum on one outfit.

At this, Mr. Marcus smiled and said to the saleswoman, "Go ahead and have the dress fitted. Betty is our little girl as well as her parents', and we want her to be the prettiest girl at the ball. Charge her the cost price, and everyone will be happy."

I feel Mr. Marcus's generosity was partially prompted by Will's family connection with Minnie, Marcus's wife. Will had told me that as a boy he had sat in a buggy outside the Mittenthal house waiting for his mother, who was inside giving nonprofessional assistance to the doctor at the birth of Minnie Mittenthal, who later married Mr. Marcus.

On the morning after the Idlewild Ball, I read in the *Dallas Morning News* that

> back in 1884, one of the belles of the day, Miss Mollie Betterton, suggested the name "Idlewild" for a recently organized bachelor's club. Fifty-four years have gone by and still the Idlewild Ball opens the social season, but now it is with a magnificent splendor. Because there were nineteen attractive girls to introduce to society, the largest number of debs of any year's record, together with the extreme beauty of the ballroom, the 1938 Idlewild chapter stands ahead of its other balls, brilliant tho they were. The debutantes were . . .

Will and I followed the customary rules and gave a large daytime party to introduce Betty to my older friends and a dinner dance at the Baker Hotel for the debutantes. Betty's father, because of his pride in his favorite daughter, enjoyed both the Idlewild Ball and her dinner dance, but later took great care to be out of town for all the other evening invitations, and I was forced to go with various friends.

The Terpsichorean Ball ended the formal debutante season. Betty, in spite of her reluctance to become a debutante, had had a very enjoyable winter, particularly since it had given her the opportunity to renew friendships with the younger set of Dallas, with whom she had largely lost contact during her four years of college.

During most of the winter social season, Betty's friends from Oklahoma City, Tom Slick and his sister Betty, had been in Dallas. Tom was a handsome and well-mannered youngster, but for some reason I did not feel too comfortable with him. Betty had been introduced to Tom during her freshman year at Vassar while he was a student at Yale, and they had dated constantly during their college years. I seemed to feel instinctively that Betty would eventually marry him and that he was not the right man for her. The Sunday following the Terpsichorean Ball Betty's engagement to Tom was announced. Very shortly Tom's mother wrote inviting Betty and me to Oklahoma City to meet some of her friends and to make plans for the wedding. Because of the family's financial position and their wide acquaintance in the oil industry, she presented a guest list of about three thousand people, scattered far and wide throughout the country. That was not the kind of wedding I had in mind for my first daughter, but I set out to comply with her wishes.

Having had no church membership for a long time, we selected the Highland Park Methodist Church for the wedding, not as a matter of preference, but simply because it was a beautiful church, and its seating capacity was adequate.

Apparently I was the only member of either family who was unhappy over the coming alliance. Both my husband and my father were pleased that Betty was marrying somebody who could care for her in luxury all of her life.

Only a few weeks later I was awakened one night by my mother's frantic calling from the downstairs door at the side of the house. When I reached her, her only cry was, "Your father wants you, your father wants you." Both Will and I hastened next door to find that my father had suffered a severe heart attack, from which he died the following afternoon.

All of the wedding plans were canceled and the date postponed for a week. When it did occur, it was a simple home ceremony with only the family and a few intimate friends present. I remember well standing alone with tears in my eyes at the small Love Field airport. A member of Tom's family by marriage walked up and said, "It was a beautiful little wedding in spite of the sad circumstances that preceded it, but I must add that in all my years of experience, you are the unhappiest mother-in-law I have ever seen."

I was relieved that Will had not been as observant. It would have disturbed him greatly, for he was too firm in his belief that no girl could be anything but happy when married to one of the few heirs to a reputed seventy-five-million-dollar fortune.

17

Anne had graduated in June, 1939, from Sarah Lawrence and, like Betty, was planning to make her debut at the Idlewild Ball in the fall. Anne's debut closely followed the pattern of Betty's; the ball itself was beautiful and enjoyed by all. Will and I entertained for her exactly as we had for her older sister. Unlike Betty, she was not elected the most popular debutante; however, she was selected by the Terpsichorean Club to lead the Grand March with Charles E. Long, Jr., the club president. At the end of the debutante season she did not marry; instead, together with her best friend, Anne accepted a position running Bill McFadden's Gift Shop.

Her father's reaction to this was exactly the same as it had been when Betty proposed working at the wayward girls' house in New York City. Anne, however, continued with her plans and worked happily until the next fall, when she was invited to be the Duchess from Dallas in the Battle of Flowers in San Antonio. While there, she was introduced to Billy Gibbons, the son of a well-known Houston family.

Billy and Anne were married in the Church of the Incarnation on October 3 the following year. The wedding was exceptionally beautiful because Billy's cousin was the officiating minister, and certain privileges were given for decorating the altar and church. After a two week's honeymoon, the couple settled in Houston.

Anne's wedding was soon followed by the announcement of the engagement of our son, William, to Vera Noland, a Clarendon girl. Because Clarendon was small and any kind of entertaining there was difficult, Will and I planned to give the rehearsal dinner at our local home. Since caterers were not available, poor Maude had to prepare the food—a terrible task. My contribution was to procure the champagne.

Immediately after breakfast on the day before the rehearsal, I began to dress in order to get an early start to Amarillo. As usual, Mona Chamberlain was going with me and her son, Kelly, would drive the car. Noticing that I was already dressing, Will asked, "What on earth are you planning to do at this early morning hour?"

"Mona and I are going to Amarillo to buy the champagne," I replied. "I knew you were busy and didn't want to ask you to make the trip."

"Don't you and Mona know," he quickly responded, "that after leaving Amarillo you will be back in dry territory? The whiskey store is under constant watch by the police, and you will be arrested and your purchases confiscated before you are more than two miles out of town, so why go on a wild goose chase?"

I laughed and said, "I remember well all the things you've told me and the difficulty of getting the liquor into dry territory, but I have a plan, a good plan. I'll get the champagne, so don't worry, and both the champagne and I shall return home without a bit of trouble. Just wait and see."

"All right, go ahead," he answered. "God knows what kind of fool idea you have in your head, but I know there is no need to waste my time attempting to stop you. I shall make one change in my plans, however. I shall remain at the bank all day instead of going to the ranch, so when you get arrested, call me, and I'll come get you out of whatever trouble you are in."

When I told Mona all Will had said, she laughed and answered, "Maybe I have more respect for your ideas than Will does. In any case, don't tell Kelly and me anything. Just take us along, and we shall be interested bystanders all the way."

So we drove happily on to Amarillo, purchased two cases of champagne, and ordered them placed in the trunk of the car. As we sat down, I turned to Kelly and said, "Unless I am badly mistaken, a policeman is watching and waiting from the car over yonder in readiness to follow us out of town. Pay no attention to him, but get us to the sheriff's office as quickly as possible."

Luckily, Kelly knew where the designated office was, and very shortly I was standing before the sheriff's desk. "By way of introduction," I said, "I'm Mrs. William J. Lewis of Dallas and Clarendon, Texas. Here is my checkbook for identification. I'm certain you know my husband."

He nodded in agreement as I continued, "I've come to ask a big favor of you. Our son, William, and Vera Noland are to be married on Saturday. My husband and I are giving the rehearsal dinner tomorrow evening in Clarendon. I have in my car two cases of champagne with which to toast the bride and groom at the party. I know that I am taking it into dry territory, but I feel sure that since you now know both my husband and me, you will be aware that we are not going to attempt to sell any of it. So, and I hope you will agree with me, I should like some kind of verification to show whoever stops us on the way."

With a broad smile, the sheriff arose and shook his head, saying, "It has not only been a pleasure to meet Will Lewis's wife, but also a pleasure to meet a woman with as much common sense as you. It will give me the greatest pleasure to supply you with an escort to see that you not only get out of Amarillo, but into Clarendon and home without the least bit of trouble."

We arrived home about four in the afternoon, and I rushed into the house, calling, "Will, are you here? If you are, please hurry out to our car and thank the nice policeman who escorted us home and help him get the champagne into the house."

Will tarried only long enough to hear all I had told him, then stopped and said, "You're the craziest woman I have ever known, and I'll never understand you. I'll bet there is not another woman in Texas who could have dreamed up such a fool idea in the first place, and then, to cap it all, gotten away with it."

William and Vera's wedding was simple, as was to be expected in a town no larger than Clarendon. As soon as the postnuptial breakfast was over, the bride and groom left by car for New Orleans, where they planned to spend their honeymoon.

18

WILLIAM and Vera did not reach their destination. They were only several hundred miles down the road when the Sunday announcement of the attack on Pearl Harbor came on the air. They turned around to start homeward as quickly as possible. The war, which had been underway in Europe for two years or more, had suddenly become America's war.

William, fully aware of his father's opposition to his enlisting, made no attempt to volunteer during the first few months. In time, however, he went to Amarillo to enlist in the navy. He did not have the two years of college required for officer training, but in his case an exception was made because his freshman grades had been so high. William returned to Amarillo a few weeks later to await instructions about his commission and where he would be sent for training. On his final trip, he was informed that the navy did not want him after all, because he was making a far greater contribution as manager of a large ranch than he would make as a junior officer.

Although Will never discussed the matter with me, I feel certain he had taken steps to prevent William's enlistment. Like any other mother, I was greatly relieved to have the security of knowing that our son would never be in the battle zone. But understanding William's nature, I realized that he would suffer a disastrous effect in his future life if he remained in the security of home while all of his friends left to fight—and I was correct in my judgment. In time, the husbands of all three of his sisters served either in the army, the navy, or the air corps, and William never remained in the room when the war was discussed.

Before the war was over, our family, including the girls' husbands, came to represent almost every characteristic and activity of a nation in the turmoil of fighting for its life. One preferred to fight, but was not allowed to; the family of another made every effort to prevent his being drafted; a third was too old for the draft, but did not care to stay behind while many of his friends were at the battlefront; and one was intelligent enough to see that war was inevitable and prepared himself to become a volunteer officer rather than a drafted foot soldier.

The story of the family's involvement in the war begins far afield with John Young, who had been Betty's sweetheart during her high school years and was destined to become her second husband. At this time, England and Germany had been at war for about a year. The draft had been reinstated in the United States, and most of the general public, as well as the War Department, had come to the conclusion that it was only a matter of time until America would be forced to join in the fight.

In the winter of 1940, John returned to Dallas and, with the assistance of certain Southern Methodist University professors, completed the course of study required for acceptance in the air corps at Fort Sill, Oklahoma. At about this same time, Joan returned from Vassar. Very quickly she informed her father that, irrespective of the family's objections, she was not going to return east in the fall, but instead planned to register at the University of Texas in Austin. Shortly after she entered the university, a young man from Corsicana, Kay Tatum, became her favorite date.

On December 7, 1941, Pearl Harbor was attacked. On the day following the attack, Kay absented himself from school long enough to enlist in the Army Air Corps. Upon his return he told Joan, with his customary good humor, that he did not want her to get the impression he was either overly brave or desirous of fighting for his country. Instead, he said, he had enough sense to realize that since his family was well known in Corsicana, and since he would not be twenty-one for several weeks, he would very likely be the first draft choice made in his hometown. He had decided, therefore, that if he were to fight, he would do it not as a foot soldier but as a pilot.

The following March, Tom and Betty left for Washington, D.C., where Tom had been given a job as one of the numerous "dollar-a-year" men without any official position. This was arranged through Tom's mother and stepfather, who were an extremely wealthy couple. Several years before Betty met Tom, his stepfather had been kidnapped. The story of the kidnapping does not belong here, so we shall only say that it was solved in a most unusual manner by the victim of the kidnapping himself. In the numerous and general investigations that followed, Tom's parents grew to know extremely well many politicians and high officials in Washington. During this time, Tom's mother was developing not only a more protective attitude toward her entire family, but also a strong belief that her son was in a stratum above those who were being called on to fight for their country; as a result, she was determined to prevent his being placed in active service. Tom's family quickly discovered, however, that his job as a dollar-a-year man was too transparent; he was then assigned to the Board of Economic Warfare in Santiago, Chile.

By the spring of 1943, two important things had happened to Betty. She had become pregnant and, because of the lack of proper medical attention in Santiago and her unhappiness with her marriage to Tom, had decided to come home. Soon after arriving in Texas, she was notified by Tom that since he was going to be drafted anyway, he was ready to enter the Naval Officers' Training School. Betty's first child, William, was born in August that same year, and Tom left for training shortly afterward. After a short period as Tom's wife, Betty started divorce proceedings and again came home with her small son to live.

Meanwhile Anne's husband, Billy, who was over thirty, enlisted and was sent to officers' training school in Florida. During his absence Anne also returned home and while there gave birth to their first child, Billy, Jr. After finishing his training in Florida, Billy was assigned to the office of the flying school in Stamford, Texas, where Anne and her baby joined him for a short period. Billy was then assigned to Fort Worth for special training before going overseas, and once again Anne came home to have a baby, their second son, Lewis.

In the meantime, John Young had not only finished two years of combat in North Africa, but, by special request, had consented to fly the commanding officer, Colonel Cain, on the first low-level attack on the Ploesti oilfields, in Rumania, in August, 1943. After that mission he was sent back to the states, where he served as air inspector and also traveled for the government to encourage the purchase of war bonds. Early in 1945, John, too, was sent to Fort Worth, and both he and Billy came over every Sunday to spend the day.

The war also brought difficulties in other family relationships. Immediately following the death of my father in 1939, my mother had begun to show signs of approaching senility. With the assistance of our family physician, we placed her in an excellent mental hospital in Galveston. Because it was wartime, no planes were allowed to land there. To visit her I was forced to fly to Houston, where arrangements were made for me to drive to and from Galveston with the postman who carried the airmail. I remember well flying from Houston in one plane that had been gutted and had only plank seats straight down on either side. I was not only the sole woman on the plane, but was also, with the exception of the flight crew, the only white person. The plane was filled with Japanese.

Since I was the only girl in the family, most of the responsibility for the care of our mother had been left to me. I would not ever allow Will to go visit her, because by this time he was in his mid-seventies, and I felt he should not be allowed to see anyone suffering from the ravages of old age.

Throughout the various changes in our home and family brought about by the war years, I, like all my friends, was working steadily with the Dallas Red Cross. It was not until long after the war that I realized how futile had been all this expenditure of energy. At the same time, I wondered if the people who organized the war were not as stupid as the people who managed the Red Cross.

When I was selected as head of the Red Cross canteen kitchen, I was required to obtain a health certificate from the city before taking over the job. The following morning, I went to City Hall. Upon stating my mission, I was told it was not necessary to see the doctor—the nurse could handle the matter easily. In a few minutes, a nurse entered the room and said, "Lift up your skirt above your knees." After a pause she added, "I see no swelling," and made out my health certificate. The nurse evidently did not know that syphilis does not always make the knees swell, and, to be exact, a blood test should have been given.

I held my job with the Red Cross for a year or so, after which the canteen was moved to Love Field. When I discovered that we were destined to serve only officers, I resigned. I believed that there were far more privates than officers in the war and that it was the height of bad taste and lack of judgment for a charitable organization to bestow its benefits only on commissioned men.

In June of 1943, Joan graduated Phi Beta Kappa from the University of Texas and returned home. She informed us that she had taken flying lessons while in Austin and had already contacted the Lou Foote Flying School in Oak Cliff. School officials had told her that if she flew well enough to pass the test, they would employ her as a flying instructor. She worked at this job for quite some time and even bought a small airplane in partnership with one of the mechanics. Many of her pupils were students from the nearby naval flying school. Whenever flying became too difficult for them, they took extra lessons from Joan. Although I was fearful over her being in the air constantly, I was pleased that she had something to occupy her time. Unlike her sisters, she was unable to make a debut because the Idlewild Ball was canceled during the war years.

The confusion and turmoil of the last few years had been indescribable. Of the three girls, Joan had always been the closest to me, and only a few weeks after she returned to

Dallas she discovered that the war years had been too much for me and that I was almost at the breaking point.

Joan wrote our family physician, who at this time was serving as an officer in the medical corps of a large hospital in Utah. He suggested a psychiatrist in Denver; the appointment was quickly made, and Will and I left to see him. Will reacted to my going to the psychiatrist in his usual undemonstrative manner. He made no comment and asked no questions, but offered willingly to drive me to Denver, saying he would remain there until he saw me nicely settled.

On Dr. Rymer's initial visit he talked first to Will alone, but only for a few minutes. When he called me in, he said, "I have suggested that your husband return home immediately and that he not contact you again while you are here. As for myself, I could not work with him very well, because his only answer, when I asked why you were ill, was, 'I do not have the slightest idea, because I give her everything she wants.'"

The doctor suggested that I spend a month in Denver, at a certain hotel at the edge of Jackson Park, where I would find comfortable surroundings and congenial companionship. I was also to walk two miles every day and study the literature he would give me.

At the end of the month I returned home, not only improved in health but with a far better understanding of the manner in which the wise person faces with composure the varied and numerous problems in life. Will paid a very large bill without question. Never once after my return home nor during the seventeen remaining years of his life did he allude to my experience with the psychiatrist.

19

GERMANY surrendered on May 8, 1945. On August 6, an American pilot dropped the first atomic bomb on Hiroshima, Japan. The second bomb fell on Nagasaki three days later. Such a devastating, horror-filled course of action would never have been considered by a civilized nation except on the premise that it would quickly end the war with Japan, which, in turn, would save the lives of as many Japanese soldiers as American G.I.s. Japan quickly admitted defeat, and the long years of war were ended.

Although the war was officially over in August of 1945, it had not quite ended for our family. Billy Gibbons was ordered to the Philippines, and Anne and her two boys came home to remain until his discharge from the army the following spring. Betty had received her divorce, and John finished with his army career, returning to Dallas to live. They were soon married and settled in a small house that Will had helped them buy.

By this time I was in my early fifties, Will had reached his mid-seventies, and we had been married over thirty years. William was managing the business well under his father's strict supervision, and Will remained at home in Dallas a great part of the time.

Although Will retained his good mind to the end and was at that time still occasionally cutting cattle from the herd, I could see evidence of the changes of approaching old age. One of the most important changes concerned our home in Dallas.

The pressures brought about by the war, numerous babies and small children, the enlargement of the family circle, and the disruption of the servants' regular routine had resulted in much confusion. Our house and garden were practically in a shambles. The neighborhood had deteriorated badly over the years. Most of our friends had long since settled in a beautiful new addition to the west of us known as Highland Park, and apartments were already rising on our street. The house next door had recently been sold and was converted by the new owners into a boardinghouse. Among the boarders was a motorcycle officer, and our days and nights were interrupted by police calls from his motorcycle radio. One morning in the fall of 1945, Will looked up from his breakfast coffee and said without preamble, "Find a good real estate salesman. The time has come for us to move."

Because I had not achieved happiness for either Will or myself in planning the house on Swiss Avenue, and because I hesitated to inquire about the size and quality of our newly proposed home, I was careful in the houses I chose to take Will to see. After leaving the second house I was considering, he turned to me and, in a slightly irritated voice, inquired, "Do you think it is my intention, since all the children will soon be away from home, to place you in a dump for the rest of your life? Tell the agent to show us a good house."

The one we finally purchased was on Belfort Place, a short street that ran into Armstrong Parkway, Highland Park's most prestigious avenue. Will had apparently recovered from the drought and, for some unknown reason, seemed willing to go to any expense to change the house into everything the decorator suggested and I wished for.

In the end it became the home that suited our style of life beautifully, exactly the kind of home I had always wanted. My favorite room was the paneled library with its filled bookshelves and glassed-in fireplace overlooking the garden, which was surrounded by walls of very old, handmade pink brick. Fu dogs guarded the entrance to the small patio, where a Kuan Yen statue arose from a fountain bowl of lotus leaves. Once again, we were living in the kind of home Will was proud of, and I never ceased to thank him for such an unexpected gift. Although I had always felt I did not belong in the

Swiss Avenue house, my feelings about the Belfort Place house were exactly the opposite.

We moved into the house in the late spring, just in time to announce the engagement of Joan to Kay Tatum, who had recently finished his extended tour of duty as a flight officer in the Indo-China theater. The wedding would take place in the fall.

A few months before the move, Maude, who had helped me rear all of our children and who was very close to us, died from cancer. We tried first one cook and then another without any success until Jean, Maude's daughter, suggested that we "make do" until her daughter, Wilma, finished her second year of college; Wilma would then become the housemaid, and Jean would take over the cooking.

Thinking of all Maude had meant to us, I said to Will, "I do not think we showed sufficient appreciation to Maude. Let's not make the same mistake with Jean. Let us start out by procuring for her a home in her name." Will was more than agreeable. We bought the house with a good down payment, and Jean paid a small monthly payment for about two years. Suddenly one day, to Jean's surprise, Will went to the mortgage company, paid the remaining debt in full, and, returning home with a broad smile, handed the deed to Jean.

I was especially pleased because Wilma was Maude's granddaughter, which meant that I was acquiring the third generation of a family that had supplied my chief servants much of our married life. This proved to be an excellent arrangement, for we also had a good chauffeur who, as is customary in Texas, did both yardwork and housework and served in the dining room.

During that same spring of 1946, two other important events transpired. Several years earlier, Will had formed a small partnership with an old-time R.O. cowboy, Shortie Rorie, in order to purchase 33,000 acres of the famous Mill Iron tract and to set up another small ranch. After several years of partnership Will bought Shortie out, the partnership was dissolved, and Will began the legal arrangements to sell this ranch to our three girls. By the end of 1946, the last payment on the ranch had been made, and it became our daughters' property.

At about the same time, Will instituted plans to sell the Shoe Bar Ranch to William. Because my name was required on the papers for these transactions, I was well aware of all that was going on. I never asked a question or made any comment, although I well remember secretly resenting the fact that Will considered it proper to turn 56,000 acres over to our son, while dividing 33,000 acres among the three girls. I do not know whether I have an excessive amount of pride, or whether I took offense when no offense was intended. In any case, in our nearly fifty years of marriage, I never, after Will's early rebuffs, inquired again about anything connected with his business.

Will had two or three main purposes in life; the chief one, to succeed financially. I hasten to explain here that Will said to me many times, "It is not really my wish to have all the money in the world. I only want to be certain that I make a good trade each time, and that my cattle when sold make a nice percentage profit on my year's work." I also believe, although he never admitted it, that he subconsciously wished all his financial success to be attached to the Lewis name.

Excessive income taxes, the capital gains tax, and the Social Security system were introduced to Will very late in his life, and he had no patience with any of them. As a result, he set out to arrange a system to place as much of his property as possible into his children's hands before he died. All of this was done according to law. Will was never the least bit dishonorable. Furthermore, he wanted the sale to be permanent, so it was all handled in a very strict fashion under the supervision of a fine lawyer. He was very wise about this, because he was managing the various ranches in order to sell them on time, so the children could pay him back gradually. I have no specific memory of Will ever discussing with me anything as important as giving a ranch to a child; I always had the idea, however, that he gave William the ranch as a guarantee that William would handle the family business without pay.

One evening, to my surprise, he said, "I went this morning to the office of your friend, Hart Willis, to change my will. Among several other things, I willed my half of the house to the children in order to avoid the double tax."

I looked at him speechlessly for a few minutes and then said, in a very quiet voice, "I know, Will, that I did not contribute to the fortune you have made, and I know that it is your privilege to do with your possessions what you desire. But for once I feel required to tell you my reaction to what you have just told me. If you die before me, which is highly probable since you are twenty-two years older, I will have packed my clothes before I take you to Clarendon for the funeral, in order to be ready when I return to Dallas to go directly to a hotel, because never for one night do I intend to live in a house of which my children own half." Will did not reply, but shortly thereafter removed the change.

On September 14, 1946, Joan and Kay were married. The wedding was very beautiful.

20

SHORTLY after Will suggested that we needed a new home, he made another suggestion that equally surprised me. During our long years of marriage, we had traveled very little, although he had told me many times, "I shall be glad to pay to send you, the children, and a nurse on a long trip to Europe any time you wish to go, as long as I do not have to accompany you." So it was with astonishment that I heard him say one morning at breakfast, "The children are gone now, Bill, and William is managing the ranch satisfactorily under my direction. I remember returning home from Clarendon one afternoon, during the period when there was a racetrack between Dallas and Fort Worth, and finding you, Sallie Windrow, and Elma Knight having a very pleasant afternoon betting through a bookie on the horse races."

Will went on to say that he knew I had frequently attended the races with our good friends, the Robert Cowarts, and had learned to like the sport immensely. After thinking it over a great deal, he said, he wished to ask a special favor of me: to promise that never again, as long as I lived, would I place a bet with a bookie. Horse racing, Will warned me, can easily become an addiction, for the combination of telephone and bookie makes racetrack betting possible at any moment of the day or night. Because I agreed to his request, Will promised to start taking me every summer and winter to the horse races in California.

"We shall stay in a beautiful hotel, have a long vacation away from home, and do something that both you and I will enjoy," Will finished. "We shall write a hotel in Pasadena, make reservations immediately for the first of January, and spend a month watching the races at the Santa Anita track."

In Pasadena, California, we stayed at the Huntington, which at that time was possibly one of the largest and most beautiful family hotels in America. On its staff was a hostess whose business it was to see that everyone was entertained and that no one was left alone. The Santa Anita track was also run on a very high standard, with fine horses and the finest jockeys in America. We occupied a box that belonged to the hotel and was ideally situated. We then joined the Turf Club, which adjoined the general admission grandstand. The service and the food there were both excellent.

The following summer we joined the Del Mar Turf Club and made reservations at the La Valencia Hotel in La Jolla. La Jolla was a small but beautiful seacoast town. Flowers grew everywhere, and even the yards of the cottage houses were ablaze with color. Many Dallas people, among them a few of our close friends, returned summer after summer, as did Will and I.

Like all racing fans, we spent hours studying the racing forms. Will was an excellent judge of horses and placed his bets intelligently. I, on the other hand, had more fun following various systems. For instance, if I lost for several days while betting on horses that, according to the racing form, should have won, I changed over to the "long shots" suggested by the newspaper, which was most successful. For years I suspected that the man responsible for this particular list of long shots had a racetrack companion who informed him when a probable agreement had been made among the jockeys. I began by betting five dollars to win, then adding another five to each bet until I brought in a long shot. Occasionally this required more than one day and caused the amount that was bet to exceed my customary wager on a single race.

I happened to be playing this system one summer when William and Vera were visiting us. Luckily for me, a long shot upon which I had a substantial bet came in. As I returned to the table with about eight hundred dollars spread out in my hand, the waiter happened to be serving our luncheon. On seeing the money, he said with a little hesitation, "Madam, please do not take offense when I ask you how you happened to choose a horse that no one else at the track thought had a chance to win?"

Before I could answer, our son, who by this time happened to have a small racing stable of his own, quickly replied, "She could not possibly tell you, for she really knows nothing about horses. She is simply the luckiest woman I have ever known. She seems to succeed at almost everything she attempts."

During our early days at Del Mar, the now-famous Willie Shoemaker was a seventeen-year-old jockey learning to ride. Even in the beginning, he had a wonderful way with horses. What attracted my attention was that he rarely used his whip, and many times I heard other spectators say, as he drew near the finish line, "Watch Willie talk his horse in to win."

One summer I did not bet on a single horse; I bet instead on the jockey, Shoemaker. I did not do so, however, if the odds were too low or if he occupied a post position that I considered either too close in or too far out. At one point in the summer I was ahead about fifteen hundred dollars. Later, however, I lost a few hundred. At this point I hasten to add that betting on horse races is not an amusement for profit. Nor can the average racetrack better be taken literally when he tells you he has won. There were any number of summers when both Will and I came out several hundred dollars the loser.

I remember one season at Santa Anita when I refused to bet during the last ten days because I was ten or twelve hundred dollars in the hole. This irritated Will very much, and he would begin each day by saying, "You must remember that if we were in New York it would cost far more than that to dine out and go nightly to the theater." He added, "I remind you of the little trip to New York you took with Joan and Kay. *My Fair Lady* had opened a few weeks before, and if I remember correctly, you were forced to pay a scalper forty or fifty dollars apiece for your tickets."

Will and I enjoyed nine years of California vacations together. It was a wonderful way for a semi-invalid and a woman who was no longer young to amuse themselves. I feel certain that one reason I enjoyed it so much was that except for the theater, which Will always liked, whether live theater or moving pictures, horse racing was the only other amusement from which we derived equal pleasure.

The hotel guests, particularly at the Huntington in Pasadena, came either from the Eastern Seaboard or from Canada, and they were charming, intelligent, and amusing. Both Will and I enjoyed them, and it often interested me greatly to watch him talk and laugh with them after dinner or during the races while sharing the same box. I remembered, as I watched him, that he was never as free and easy at home, and I never saw him enjoy his social contacts in Dallas in the same free and talkative manner as he did at the Huntington.

The California vacations and the beautiful new home on Belfort made these years one of the happiest periods of our life. Of course, during these years many other things happened, not all of them pleasant.

Shortly after we moved into the Belfort Place house, Will discovered that the lot directly behind us was for sale. He quickly purchased it and suggested to Betty and John that they sell their cottage on Greenbriar and, with his help, build on the lot the kind of house their family would need. Betty was again pregnant and was destined quickly to have another child, which increased the number of her children to four. The following year their new home on Rheims Place was completed, and Will and I were living happily, with our oldest daughter well established within a stone's throw of our house.

During this decade, the size of our family grew steadily. As our daughters' needs increased, Will continued to be generous until all three were finally settled in commodious homes of sizes suited to their families. Unfortunately, our son never had any children. I had often wondered if it were a source of sorrow to Will to know that his name was destined to be lost, particularly because he would have been so proud of some of his grandsons. The subject was never mentioned between us, however. As time moved on, William, with his close business ties with his father and the Shoe Bar doing so well, needed no financial assistance in providing a good home for Vera and himself.

The normal circumstances of these years were occasionally interrupted by tragic events. At the conclusion of the war, our family physician had left the army to return to his practice—not in Dallas, but in the smaller town of Gainesville, some one hundred miles distant. We immediately moved Mama to Gainesville to the hospital where our doctor practiced. I remember well the long drives I made alone to see her and the deep sorrow with which I watched eyes that remained blank and a mouth from which the sound of words never came.

Upon my mother's death in 1951, I asked Will what her long illness had cost him. He quickly replied, "About $140,000, but what difference did that make? Why wouldn't I be willing to care for your mother in the same manner I would have cared for mine, had it been necessary?"

In the years immediately following, Will progressed to eighty and beyond and weakened slowly. It gave him endless pleasure to know that his favorite child, Betty, and her four children were living immediately behind us and that John, her husband, was acquiring a position of importance in the banking world.

21

In September, 1957, Billy and Anne left for Washington, D.C., to show a little of America to their oldest son, Billy, Jr., who had been entered in the Hill School at Pottstown, Pennsylvania, in preparation for going later to Duke University. At dinner that night, Billy suffered a heart attack and died within a few hours. Although Anne and Billy had been very happily married, she took his death well. When Will inquired about her needs, she reminded him that her house was paid for, that she would remain in Houston because she had been away from Dallas so long that Houston was now her home, and that Billy had left her enough to care for her well. Many months later, while visiting Betty in Dallas, Anne met Phil David, whose wife had died about the same time as Billy. They married in 1959, and Anne returned to Dallas to live.

Gradually, as the years passed, Will began more and more to show the signs of old age. We had long given up our vacation trips to California, although we were able to go twice to Arizona. Whenever Will felt he must attend to ranch business, he no longer traveled by train. Instead, I drove him, and we stayed in the old family home. As a rule, William and Vera had dinner with us in order to discuss business, which made a long ride to the ranch unnecessary.

During these last few years, except for one severe fibrillation, Will's physical symptoms were restricted to a great loss of strength and occasional short but frightening breathing attacks, when, apparently, some tiny foreign substance entered his lungs.

Will's invalidism was one of the most pathetic experiences I had ever endured; not because I objected to nursing him all the time, but because I sympathized so deeply with him. The thought haunted me that it must be a tragic experience for Will to live out his final hours in the company of one whom he had never come to understand, and in an almost foreign land, far removed from the beautiful rolling prairies and the life he had lived and loved so long. For several years I never left Will for a minute except for an occasional outing to play cards, when either Betty, who lived behind us, or Joan, who lived in Corsicana, stayed with him.

The week before he died the doctor insisted against both Will's and my wishes that Will be placed in the hospital. Within a few days our son, William, came down to see his father and told him as far as possible every detail of what was going on at the ranch. When he had finished, Will said, in a most patronizing voice, "I am certain, son, it will work out all right, but, of course, I would not have done any of it that way." It was my recognition of this characteristic in my husband that had made me fight so hard to prevent our son from going into business with him.

Will died three days later, very quietly. He simply closed his eyes and went to sleep. As he would have wished, I had his body taken to the old family house in Clarendon before burial.

That night I stood before the casket for a long time before going to my bedroom. He looked far more like a man of sixty-five than one in his early nineties. As I stood there, I wondered if he had ever regretted marrying me, for I had known for many years that I was not the kind of wife he should have had. Would he have been happier with another kind? I do not know, but I doubt it. Strange as it may seem, although he passionately loved the plains and prairies of Texas and was completely attuned to them spiritually, he himself never became a Texan. He was still the man who had been the boy from Maryland.

As I left the church at the conclusion of the funeral the next day, someone I did not know said to me, "Please look down the street. As far as you can see there are cars and buggies, and each and every one of them is owned by a man whom at one time or another your husband has helped." Will was buried in a forlorn, ill-kept, windswept West Texas cemetery a mile or so out from town.

At William's suggestion, the burial plot selected was large enough for only three graves—one for Will, one for William, and one for William's wife. By this time William and Vera knew that they would never be able to have any children and that I, unlike Will, did not want to be buried in a land so foreign to my nature. Furthermore, because I was not sufficiently attuned to their approach to life, I secretly felt with sorrow that I did not belong by the side of Will and William for eternity.

At almost ninety-two, it makes me a little sad to realize that my long and unusually blessed life appears destined to end in a world filled with war, fear, hatred, great wealth, great poverty, and a sharp decline in the moral and ethical code by which I was reared. Although I do not consider Reagan either perfect or another Solomon, I do feel strongly that his interests are for the betterment of conditions in this country and that it is the duty of every American to work with him as far as possible. It disturbs me greatly to hear of the enormous wealth and the powers that lie in the hands of a few. It also disturbs me to hear of the thousands of laborers who are out of jobs and of the thousands who do not belong but remain on government welfare.

I understand and sympathize with the woman who is forced to work and is unable to receive the same salary as the man who previously held her job, but I cannot understand the women of America who apparently wish to do a man's job, whether holding a job is necessary for them or not. Their absence from home weakens both the home and the family structure, and it has always been on the home and family that the strength of a nation was built. I am greatly concerned over our poor public school system and with the quality of the teachers; I am disturbed that many children are discovered carrying weapons and that narcotics are frequently found and sold on the school grounds; but my deepest fear lies with the promiscuity of sex and the absence of the old-fashioned belief that God made sex in order to make man and woman come to feel as one. I am beginning to wonder, however, if all the old rules by which I was reared were for the best, or if I, like many other old people, am simply unable to accommodate to the new ways.

The writing and rewriting of this little manuscript has not only revived many memories, both happy and sad, but it has also caused me to form two very firm conclusions.

First: in spite of our incompatibility, I loved Will to the end, or I would not have been so steadfast in refusing ever to allow another man to come see me during the twenty-three years since his death.

Second: had I not been a simple girl of the early twentieth century but more like the college-educated, business-minded, sophisticated girl of today, I would never have considered marrying him.

What is your opinion?